MENDIP MARINE
A Passage To War

by

John Willcox Webb
Researched by Dinah Read

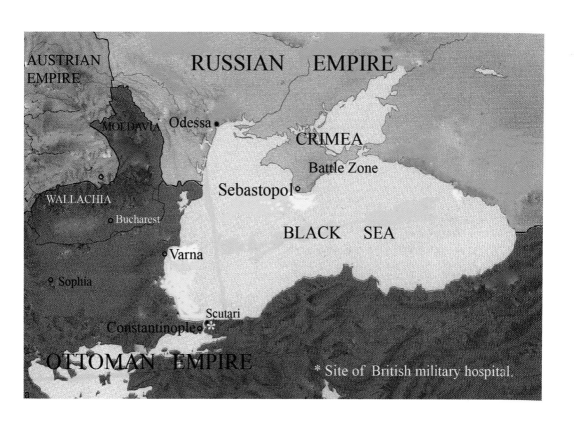

The Journal of a mid-19th Century Marine

"In these works are several 32 pounder iron howitzers, which for the most part are manned by marine artillery, as the entire heights have up to this time been occupied by 1100 Royal Marines from the fleet - as fine a body of men as you could wish to see."

Lt. Col. Somerset J. Gough Calthorpe
Crimea 1854

HMS Vengeance. *Marine Webb served on this two decker, the ship that took him to the Crimea.*
Illustration reproduced by kind permission of the National Maritime Museum, Greenwich.

Front cover: *Royal Marines in Action (Crimea)*. An illustration by Charles Stadden, reproduced by kind permission of the Royal Marines Museum.

Back Cover: *Marine Webb was entitled to both medals depicted. The medal on the left is the British Crimean War Medal with Balaclava and Sebastopol clasps to which Marine Webb was also entitled. The other medal was issued to all allied personnel by the Turkish authorities. There were design differences in the medals issued to Sardinian, French and British personnel, but many of the British were issued with the Sardinian or French medal. This was due to the loss, by shipwreck, of the bulk of the medals designed specifically for the British.*

MENDIP MARINE
A Passage To War

by

John Willcox Webb

Researched by Dinah Read

Introduction and Editing Ken Griffiths

Book Design and Graphic Editing Rosie Tomlinson
Typing Services Elaine Griffiths
Cover Design and Maps Roy Gallop

FIDUCIA ✿ PRESS

ISBN 978 0 946217 37 3

CONTENTS

Ship of the Line leaving Cork for the Crimea

INTRODUCTION

Five years ago Dinah Read, a retired teacher, came across a journal of a mid-nineteenth century Royal Marine. His name was John Willcox Webb, the son of a Mendip farmer of modest means. John completed a ten year engagement in the service that included action in the Crimean War. His account of life in the marines is unique because there are so few personal experiences recorded by 'other ranks' of the period (or before). This is understandable given the lack of educational opportunities available to the bulk of the population. John however did have access to learning and as Dinah put it, was 'functionally literate.'

The journal ends abruptly in August 1853 during the build up of allied forces preparing for war with Russia. That John served in the war is not in doubt, as Dinah's diligent research reveals. No personal accounts of John's time in the war zone are recorded or recalled by third parties. Dinah gives possible reasons for this, one being that he found the recall of his experiences too painful. John was present at the Battle of Balaclava and the prolonged Siege of Sebastopol. The unnecessary sufferings of the troops during the first winter of 1854/5 is well recorded, as are the casualty statistics. Modern soldiers suffering from battle stress are often encouraged to talk of their experiences, even to write about them as a form of therapy, but this does not work for everyone. Throughout the ages soldiers have coped with their painful memories by trying not to recall them, hoping they will fade with time. Given the disastrous nature of the campaign and the appalling hardships John must have endured it would not be surprising if he did not wish to recollect his war time experiences in writing.

During her research Dinah built up a respect for this Mendip marine, just one of the thousands caught up in events they had no control over. Whilst the 'major players', usually the rich and/or powerful are recorded in history we hear little of the pawns who are affected by their policies. For this reason Dinah, who I think developed a soft spot for John during her research, felt that this journal should be published, as a form of memorial to him. Fiducia Press is happy to oblige. Dinah lists poetry as one of her interests and two of her poems about John have been included in Appendix 2.

Although Dinah does give a description of the Crimean campaign as John would have experienced it, I believe it is appropriate to give a brief and general account of the Crimean conflict.

A Brief and General History of the Crimean War
The seeds of the Crimean War (1853-1856) were sown in the eighteenth century when Turkey was in decline. The Russians had established themselves on the Black Sea and a weakened Turkey entered into the Treaty of Kuchuk Kainardji in 1774. Included in this treaty were ambiguous rights of intervention in the affairs of Christian subjects of the Sultan. In 1853 the Russians sought to exercise these rights and used the rejection of their demands by Turkey as justification to occupy Moldavia and Wallachia.

The British at this time saw the preservation of the Ottoman Empire as vital to the defence of India and it was only a matter of time before Britain became involved. On 4th October 1853 Turkey declared war on Russia which began badly for Turkey when Russia won a naval victory off Sinope Harbour. Anxious now at Russia's belligerency Britain in partnership with France declared war on Russia on 28th March 1854. In June of that year the allies joined the Turkish forces in Varna. Following the Russian withdrawal across the Danube a British expeditionary force under Lord Raglan, combined with a French force, landed in the Crimea on 14th September 1854. By 20th September they were engaged in the Battle of the Alma where they defeated a Russian force of 40,000. The price of this victory however was very high, the British suffering 2,000 casualties. The allies then lay siege to Sebastopol and an attempt by the Russians to relieve the siege led to the Battle of Balaclava on 25th October. They were repelled in a bloody encounter that included the disastrous Charge of the Light Brigade under Lord Cardigan. On the 5th November the Russians tried again to lift the siege, this time at Inkerman but were defeated in an even bloodier engagement. The war then stagnated into the Siege of Sebastopol, the troops suffering much hardship during the winters of 1854/1855. Poorly supported in terms of supply and reinforcements the allied army began to experience the effects of low morale.

It was at this stage of the war that newspaper reporters, particularly W. H. Russell of *The Times* began to inform the public of the plight of the troops and exposing the military incompetence of their commanders and the seemingly casual disregard by the government for the troops' welfare. Roger Fenton, who was probably the world's first accredited war photographer, recorded some aspects of the campaign but his photographs did not reveal the rough end of war; this was left to the pen of W. H. Russell. The political contacts of the nurse Florence Nightingale (who ran a hospital at Scutari in Turkey) also played their part in building up a sense of public outrage at the conduct of the war.

In January 1855 the radical politician John Roebuck tabled a motion to support a committee of enquiry into the prosecution of the whole Crimean campaign; this led to the fall of the government. Steps were then taken to improve the general management of the war, particularly in the field of logistics.

By April 1855 these reforms (including military reforms) improved the flow of supplies to the front line in time for the onset of winter. In February 1855 the British Army was is-

Barracks at Scutari - The British Hospital

sued with the new Pattern 1853 Enfield Rifle-Musket which increased accuracy at greater distances. There was a further full scale battle on 16th August 1855 when a Russian army of 57,000 men attacked a combined force of French and Sardinian troops at Tchernaya. The Russians were repulsed after a savage engagement that involved hand to hand fighting. Captain Godman of the 5th Dragoon Guards visited the battlefield the following day and recorded that ….

I rode over the ground just after; it is a terrible sight when the excitement is over to see men torn in messes by round shot and shell, and then the wounded moaning and dying all round. If king's ministers could see a few such sites I think countries would not be hurried into war.

Sebastopol was taken by the allies in September 1855, but they failed to take the dockyards and the war continued through a second winter. Sergeant Gowing of the Royal Fusiliers described the scene that confronted him as he entered Sebastopol….

The horrors inside the town, where the enemy had established their hospitals, baffle all description. Some of our non-commissioned officers and men went into those places and described scenes as heart rending and revolting in the extreme. Many of the buildings were full of dead and dying mutilated bodies, without anyone to give them a drink of water. Poor fellows, they had well defended their country's cause and were now left to die in agony, unattended, uncared for, packed as closely as they could be stowed away, saturated in blood, and with the crash of exploding forts all around them. They had served the Tsar but too well; there they lay, in a state of nudity, literally rolling in their blood. Our officers and men, both French and English found their way there indiscriminately, and at once set to work to relieve them. Medical aid was brought as quickly as possible to them, but hundreds passed beyond all earthly appearance.

In November the Royal Engineers destroyed the naval dockyards, thereby removing any threat from the Russian navy in the Black and Mediterranean Seas.

Meanwhile, a less dramatic campaign in the Baltic was being pursued by the Royal Navy, but in the end proved to be more decisive in bringing the war to a conclusion. The navy constructed what can only be described as a floating siege train of over 300 bombardment vessels with the aim of neutralising the Russian Naval base of Kronstadt. This threat forced the Russians to sue for peace and all hostilities ceased in February 1856. This was formalised by the Treaty of Paris on 30th March 1856; one of the conditions was the Russian acceptance of the neutrality of the Black Sea.

The Crimean war, even at that time, not just historically, was a by-word for wholesale incompetence and should have taught us many lessons; sadly it did not. War is still used as an instrument of foreign policy. What a change it would be and how much more satisfying if governments tried to influence events by humility and good example.

The Allied and Russian forces suffered heavy casualties during the conflict, both in dead and wounded; the source of the vast majority of deaths was disease. We can only be thankful that the Royal Navy's campaign in the Baltic was eventually successful.

But even in the midst of this carnage glimpses of humanity were revealed. There was the sensitive writing of W. H. Russell who was determined to give a truthful account of the campaign to the public, cutting through the propaganda. He was fiercely independent and not subject to restrictions as is the embedded war reporter of today; there was the heroic work of those who nursed the dying, wounded and diseased troops; there was the organizational abilities of Florence Nightingale whose work at Scutari led directly to the formation of trained nurses in Britain; and there was the work of nurse Mary Seacole, who often visited the battlefield itself to tend wounded soldiers of both sides, putting herself in the line of fire. Although largely forgotten now she was highly regarded by the troops, who feted her in Britain on their return.

Ken Griffiths.
Fiducia Press.
March 2011.

'Orion', 'Du Quesne', 'Royal George', 'Tourville', *Part of the Baltic Fleet off Kronstadt*

JOHN WILLCOX WEBB -- A MENDIP MARINE

This is the fascinating, and in many ways unlikely story of a farmer's son who for unknown reasons, and against all the odds joined the Royal Marines. It is probable that up to the time of his enlistment he had never seen the sea – let alone a ship of war. He was born at Stoke St. Michael in 1824, the fourth child of Joseph Webb. His mother Mary (nee Willcox) came from Babcary. When he was only a year or two old the family moved from Stoke to Bennets Hill Farm (originally known as Bullocks Hill). It lies just off the lane that runs down from Holcombe to Coleford beside Kilmersdon Common. There were a number of relatives living in the area, several of them innkeepers, the family name being associated with both the *Duke of Cumberland* at Edford and *The Greyhound* at Springers Hill. Joseph Webb was described in the 1851 census as a "farmer of 80 acres employing three men" although I am not sure whether he owned the farm or whether it was rented. The farmhouse still exists and is now a second home. It looks out across the valley toward Holcombe and down toward the Somerset Coal Canal. The yard and buildings at the back of the house retain some of their previous character.

My interest in the story of John Willcox Webb began when a friend placed in my hands a journal written during his service. It had long lain in a tin trunk in an attic among other family papers.This was probably not the original but a copy, made in later years. My friend who gave it to me was not able to say to whom it had belonged but thought that it had come from a great aunt, born Ann Elizabeth Purnell. It is most likely that she had been the wife and widow of the writer. In any event I was very fortunate that it had survived and that I was allowed to keep it for a year or more during which time I made my own copy. It had been written in an account book about four inches wide and eleven inches tall, leather bound and in good condition. There are one or two introductory pages and several that bear details relating to the death of friends or relatives over the years ranging from 1865 to 1874. The entries begin with his embarkation on 1st of August 1851 and end abruptly in August 1853. It may be that the original carried on beyond that date although as we shall see there are reasons why it might have been difficult to continue. The writing, though faded, is legible but too neat to have been written at sea in dark damp and cramped quarters – although the tale it tells has a flawless authenticity. I have transcribed it with great care preserving Webb's own often phonetic spelling. Webb is functionally literate and well able to express himself although he uses little or no punctuation. Capital letters indicate the emphasis that he would give to his narrative in speaking.This is in itself a charm, as it conveys the voice and manner of the man himself. He writes in the Mendip dialect as we might expect. It is likely that he learned to read at a local Methodist school. At that time the teaching method was purely phonic and consisted of learning by rote lists of related syllables, with very little opportunity to read a text. One interesting feature of the journal is that the lines are short and each one begins with a capital letter regardless of sense. This suggests that the writer may never have seen a passage in prose and may only have possessed a hymn book!

Joseph Webb, John's father was a respectable man. He was a census enumerator for the 1851 census and is recorded as having served as foreman of a jury. Certainly he was literate as apparently were most of his family, women included. We can only guess as to his qualities as a father. His son makes little reference to him in his journal and none at all to his mother but we may conclude at least that John Willcox Webb was of a decent family, had a degree of education and was not underprivileged. That he should have driven, or ridden to Warminster market on a certain Saturday is in no way remarkable but what happened there is something of a surprise.

Farmhouse where John Willcox Webb was born

How It Happened
This is how Webb himself recorded this most significant event --

"I Willcox Webb Inlisted in the royal Marines P22nd of Portsmouth Divition at Warminster on the 31st of January 1846 and I joind hed Quarters at Portsmouth Hants about the Middell of February 1846"

Warminster market was a busy place, second only to Bristol as a corn market. It was a place where there was much social interaction, an interface between the dairy farmers of Somerset and the arable farmers of Wiltshire. Webb may have been there with friends as market days were central to the social life of most farming people. He would have started out in the morning to travel the twelve or fourteen miles from home, most likely in a horse and trap and conducted any business that he had undertaken. Before starting on the journey home he would have needed a decent meal. There was in the town an Inn, now the *Weymouth Arms*, but then known as the *Drum and Monkey*. Here they provided a dinner known as a 'Farmers Ordinary' – a substantial dinner was just what he would require. It was also a place of entertainment, of laughter and good spirits – and a very likely place for recruiting parties to set up their pitch. There was apparently a recruiting drive going on at that time. Perhaps the thought of "going for a soldier" had already crossed Webb's mind. The Napoleonic wars had ended thirty or so years earlier but I can't help thinking that there must have been a few veterans of the Peninsular War, of Waterloo, or even of Trafalgar still ensconced in tap rooms and ale houses over the length and breadth of England, relaxed and quite at home, telling their often repeated tales and reliving their youthful adventures whenever they were encouraged to do so. Perhaps they were the local heroes who fed a young man's dreams. It may have been that work on the farm seemed dull and hard, that being the younger brother did not promise a great future, or that there had been arguments at home. It could even be that there was a young woman who came into the picture for good or ill. It is most likely that he would have had enough alcohol to affect his judgement. What ever the reason, John Willcox Webb was recruited that day by Sergeant Greene of the Royal Marines. After all these years I find it oddly moving to build up a picture of him from an entry in the description book.

"About 22 years old. 5ft 10ins tall. Fresh Complexion. Grey eyes and brown hair. No marks or scars. Has both suffered from and been vaccinated against smallpox. Status single. Previous employment labourer."

I cannot help wondering how the news was received at home and whether or not he regretted his commitment. Nevertheless committed he was, and he must have found his new role in life a great adventure.

Initial Training And Conditions On First Posting
Eastney Barracks was not in existence until the very end of Webb's service. A generation earlier Marines were billeted at inns and alehouses in the town. This gave rise to a good deal of drunkenness and brawling and was very bad for discipline. By the mid nineteenth century there were barracks of some sort and many of the men were also accommodated in hulks. At the same time two thirds or more of the Royals were serving at sea. Basic training took place before this. There were two branches of Marines in Portsmouth, Artillery and Light Infantry, and Webb had joined the latter. He tells us a little of his early service in the opening pages of a journal that he kept at a later stage in his career.

"I imbarked On Board H M Ship *Blazer* On the 19th of October 1846 and we steamed to Cove of Cork. Thear I landed on Spick Island. Stopped thear 3 days and Went On Board the *Radamanthus* and I stopt there for only one day and then I went on board the *Myrmidon* steamer then flag ship. In March 1847 we went to Waterford and New ross and Carrick on shure I saw two ships on fire at Cove and I saw One Wreck"

At this point in time the Royal Navy was at a crucial stage in its development. The advantages of steam were becoming more and more apparent and it was evident that the future lay in that direction, but there were also disadvantages. The Admiralty were experimenting with a number of vessels of different types and designs in an attempt to discover which would suit their particular requirements. *Rattler* and *Blazer*, *Radamanthus* and *Myrmidon* were all a part of this procedure. A steam ship may not have been at the mercy of contrary winds, or indeed of too much or too little wind, but it needed a constant supply of fuel so large coal depots had to be maintained all over the globe. Most of the early models were paddle steamers. These were difficult to manoeuvre in high seas or a gale as a list to leeward rendered the windward paddle wheel useless. The paddle box was also extremely vulnerable to enemy attack and the space it occupied made it impossible to mount a full broadside. Most ships were designed to carry sail in addition to their engines but this was unpopular with the old guard as coaling was a dirty and sometimes dangerous business. The screw propeller was eventually to solve many of these problems but in the meantime the fleet embraced all kinds of ships. Webb was to serve on the full range of vessels during his service, but I suspect from his writings that he had a preference for the old sailing ships.

That Webb should have been posted to Cork is significant. A large number of Marines were drafted to Ireland at that time. The Cobh of Cork was one of the finest natural harbours in the British Isles. A military and naval base, at any time it would have been of importance, but this was 1846 and Ireland was in the grip of a horrific famine due to the failure of the potato crop. There was a lot of unrest and disturbance throughout the country and the role of the Marines was to maintain order and enforce the law as the local militia were thought to be too sympathetic to the populace. This was a time of dispossession and misery when, being unable to pay their rent and after successive failures of the potato crop, whole families were turned out onto the road and their cottages destroyed. The government in London seemed quite indifferent to their suffering and what measures were taken to supply food and shelter through the Poor Law were totally inadequate. At the same time many of the landlords, living in England and deriving most of their income from Irish estates continued to sell for export the crop of grain from the fertile land of which they had a monopoly. In three years one third of the Irish people, who had relied on potatoes as their staple diet, died of starvation or fever, or if they could scrape together the fare many of them emigrated. In Cork alone 6,000 people were buried in three pits. Webb must have been witness to some of this and I would very much like to know what he made of it all. There are records of some Naval Officers having sufficient pity on the people that they encountered off the West coast to supply them with a little bread from the ship's stores but this was a very limited resource. The official line was that the Irish peasant was drunken and improvident and should learn to help himself. Webb was a farmer's son and would have known that crop failure from a previously unknown disease was more like an act of God. On the other hand he was from Somerset, a Protestant who had probably been brought up to dislike and distrust Catholics on principle. For much of the nineteenth century the Irish were stereotyped as a rebellious, dirty and inferior race. Webb's inclination in general was to obey orders and accept authority. It is possible that he did not think too much about it but I would like to believe that at least he had his reservations. He never makes his personal feelings obvious.

Back In 'Pompey' And Home On Leave
Whatever his feelings he was back at H.Q. by July 1847 and stayed there until the beginning of December when he was stationed on the *Victory* in Portsmouth Harbour. The *Victory* at

this time was an old ship and used as a barracks, (this being long before her restoration as a national treasure). At the same time there was recognition of her historical significance and he would have been proud to belong to her.

The next piece of information Webb gives is that ….

"On the 3rd of December 1850 then I left the *Victory* and went to Hed Quarters and I got six weeks leff and went Home and so my Friends"

It is quite likely that his friends and family noticed some changes in the man. He had seen something of the world beyond Mendip although he was destined to see much more.

On H.M.S. Vengeance To The Mediterranean Fleet

Vengeance was built at Pembroke Dockyard, launched 1834 and finally hulked in 1861. She was of the Ganges class, a fast ship capable of 12 knots. The commander of Marines was William S. Aslett who eventually achieved the rank of Major General. On the 27th August 1851 Webb joined the *Vengeance* at Spit Head, one of 170 Marines on board with 750 Officers and crew. Webb was to spend the next two years on her muster roll.

Vengeance was an old fashioned 'Ship of the Line' – a sailing ship, she carried 84 guns and was one of a succession of five naval ships to bear the name, the most recent being an aircraft carrier. Her Captain was Lord Edward Russell, third son of the Duke of Bedford and brother to the Prime Minister, Lord John Russell. This was a naval family of renown. The Commander of the ship was John Mends, who was to distinguish himself during the coming war. No doubt Webb had some feelings of excitement. He listed all the posts on the ship from Lieutenants to "Docters Meats" *(mates, a naval rank, in this case a medical orderly or assistant)*. Up to this time he had not put in a lot of sea time but now he was off to see the world aboard a fine ship, on a cruise to the Mediterranean – an exotic destination indeed to a farmer's son from Mendip.

It was at this point that Willcox Webb began to keep his journal and it was this document that has been my main source of information. The keeping of a journal or log at sea was required of some ranks from the captain downward. Official logs from the *Vengeance* still exist including Captain Russell's own and one kept by a previous Master, William Faulkner, on an earlier voyage to Arctic waters. Midshipmen always kept a journal as part of their training and preparation for their examination for lieutenant. It was a rare occurrence for a common seaman or a man in the ranks of the marines to do so. It occurs to me that Webb may have hoped to forward his career by demonstrating his ability to do so and.perhaps gain some promotion.

The marines, then as now, regarded themselves as an elite force. Their role, apart from helping to fight the ship at sea or forming a landing party to fight on shore, was to maintain order and discipline on board, acting as the ship's policemen. Webb appears to have had a healthy

HMS Victory. *Used as a barracks. Marine Webb was stationed on this ship between December 1847 and December 1850*

respect for authority. He does not easily betray his private feelings and it would have been very unwise of him to commit any unorthodox views or criticisms to paper. Nevertheless there are cryptic phrases and comments that are open to interpretation. He seems to accept flogging as part and parcel of disciplinary procedure and at a near mutiny at Plymouth during refitting he fulfilled his role conscientiously, although I think one can detect an understanding and even sympathy with the underlying causes of discontent. The amount of desertion when in a home port, and attempts to deal with it in the absence of the ship's own senior officers, is well illustrated. Webb himself was several days late in rejoining his ship after his home leave and on one occasion lost his good conduct badge for a similar offence.

Webb's brief account of home leave between his first and second voyages on *Vengeance* includes an intricate railway journey from Plymouth to Frome involving an overnight stop at Bristol, and on to Bath and Chippenham, changing again for Frome; another overnight stop there and home to Coleford in the morning. At the farm he was in holiday mood "injoying" himself at markets and out "shuting" He was of course welcomed and a centre of attraction to his less adventurous friends and neighbours. He would now be a man with stories to tell – of foreign shores and strange people. He returned to the ongoing refit and preparations for the next voyage. As soon as the ship was at sea again morale and discipline improved.

Much of the journal is very repetitive as Webb consistently recorded weather conditions and position and the ship's changes of sail and course. There were also the 'housekeeping' routines of scrubbing decks and hammocks, and washing "cloaths". Although it was not in his contract to help work the ship he nevertheless wrote of helping to steer her in rough weather. It is fascinating to see how his understanding of the principles of ship handling and navigation improved over time and with experience. He was plainly pleased and proud when the *Vengeance* gave a good account of herself in speed trials and sail handling drills in competition with others in the fleet, especially when under the Command of Admiral Curry. The frigate *Phaeton* was *Vengeance's* "buddy ship" – both friend and rival. It amuses me that while he always used a capital letter when naming a sailing ship he very rarely accorded this honour to a steamer and I cannot help thinking that he is aware of the slight when he refered to "the *turrible* (*Terrible*) steamer" who took them in tow during a flat calm.

During the late summer of 1853 the combined fleets of Britain, Turkey and France were assembled at the eastern end of the Mediterranian. There was a certain tension, a sense of excitement. Army transports were arriving. There were parades and foreign Admirals being entertained on board. Parties of officers were reconnoitring past Constantinople. There were gun drills and firework displays, deliveries of fresh provisions, even a plague of locusts that had to be shovelled overboard. A French ship went aground and it was something of a spectator sport watching attempts to refloat her.

At this point the journal abruptly came to an end. Here follows my transcript of Willcox Webb's account in full to this point using his original spelling and only an occasional amplification of his punctuation where it is necessary in the interests of clarity. I have added a few footnotes for information or comment.

Dinah Read

J. W. W . HIS BOOK
(August 27th 1851)

I Willcox Webb joind Her Majesties Ship *Vengeance* on the 27th of August 1851. This Ship carries 84 Guns 12 68 lbs and the rest 32 pounds. Our Captain is Lord Edward Russell and the Ship Carries 1 Commander 5 Lieutenants 1 Master 1 Dokter 1 Purser 1 Naval Instructer 1 Chaplan 2 Dockters meats 1 Master 1 or 2 Masters Acistanes 4 Clarks 1 or 2 Under Writers 4 meats 1 Gunner 1 Carpenter 1 Boatswain 1 Master at Arms 4 Ships Corporals 1 Ships Schoolmaster. Her fool Compliment off Officers and men when she is fool Up is 750. Off Marines 1 Captain 3 Lieutenants 4 Sergeants 4 Corporals 1 piper 1 drumer 171 Privats . Total off Marines and Marine Officers 185.

On the 28th we paid 2 Months Wages to the Ships Company. On the 29th we was getting what few things we Wanted. On the 30th we Holey Stone All Decks and We Took On Board 2 Private Gentelmen 1 off them was a brother to Our Captain. On the 31st We got Up anchors and made sail at two oclok P M for Malta. We never put inn Any Whear Befor we got Near Lisbon On the 9th of September and then we Dropt Anchor in Casco Bay for One Night . On the 10th off Sept in the morning we waid anchor and stood out to sea. On the 11th verey fine wether all Day and we passed By Cape St. Vincent. On the 12th A Verey Light Breeze. On the 13th there was A Marine Floged. He Had 30 Lashes. On the 14th fine Wether . We Do wash Cloase and Scrub Hammocks wons a week. On the 15th we past Cape trafalger and Cadiz and then we got throw the the gut off Gibralter. On the 16th we past by Cape Cadat. On the 17th we lost all the wind and *the Incounter* Steamer took us in tow. On the 18 and 19th Fine wether and fine the 20th and 21st we got A Little Wind.

At six oclok P M and Maid Sail and the Steamer Let Go Off Us But we Lost all the Wind this same Night. On the 22nd a Verey fine Morning and we got Permishon from the Captain to Bath this fornoon. We floges 2 Marines One for Being Drunk and the other for Giving Cheek to a Officer. The Same Evning the Captain of the Incounter Dined On Board Of Our Ship with Our Captain. And we Past By Majorka and Manorca the Same Evning and on the 23rd and 24th Verey Light Breezes. On the 25th A Verey fine Day. Aire Bedding and Wash Cloase the same night. On the 26th a good Breeze All Day. General Quarters to Day. On the 27th and 28th Good Breeze and we am Going from 7 to 9 Knots per Hour. On the 29th a fair wind. On the 30th We fell In with a Squall about 8 o'clok A M. It did thunder and Lightning and rain Verey Hevvy While it Lasted But that was Not Long But the Wind Carried Away Our Main topsail Sheet And Had Soon Got it in ribbons and we was Cumpeld

To Bind A nother In Its Plase. We was About 90 or 100 Miles from Malta just off Pantolina . Rain all Day at times.

But On the 1st of October 1851 Very fine All Day. In the Evning the Steamer took us in tow and we Past by Pantolina. On the 2nd we Past Gozo and the sam Evning we got to Our Morings in Malta Harbour and Made fast. On the 3rd A Verey fine Morning. Pipe hands to Bath and after Breakfast we Comenst Setting Up the riggen.Oct 4thsetting Up the riggin and Watering and Pervishoning Ship. On the 5th,Sunday. Divine Servis . On the 6th Dun Watering and Pervishoning Ship and at 5o'clok P M We Let Go of Our Morings and Saild Out Of Malta Harbour. On the 7th A fine day Morning. General Quarters. A Very fine Breeze all Day. On the 8th Very fine All Day. On the 9th In a Ded Calme. In the Night Wash cloase. On the 10th A Light Breeze and at 6 oclok P M Pipe Hands to Bathe – In a Ded Calme then just off the Isale of Cundy A Verey Large Island. On the 11th A Verey Light Breeze Holey Stone All Decks to Day. On the 12th in a Ded Calme all Day. Divine Servis In the fornoon. On the 13th A Strong Breeze All Day and We Floged 1 Marine for refusing to woork. He Had 30 Lashes.

A Very Hevvy x Swell and we am forst to ship the Main Pick Savelus (?)and secure All of Our Mess things . Then we was going from 7 to 12 knots per hour. On the 14th a good Breeze and Hevvy Swell. On the 15th A verey fine Morning and we Sited Aboka Bay that Was Whear the Battel of the Niel was fought by Nelsons fleet and the French fleet. And we got just off Alexandir and Dropt Anchor at 12 o'clok at Day. This is the Capitell Seaport town in Egypt. On the 16th a verey fine Day and Verey Hot Hear. In the evning the grand Pasha Made a Preasant to Our Ships Company of 3 Bullocks and 25 Sheep and about one hundred of Turkeys and fow-ells and Plenty of Soft Bread and Cheese and Onions and Coffee and Shuger and Many a Hundred of Aiggs [1]. On the 17th we washed Cloase and we had a Verey fine Day to Dry them. Fresh Meat to Day, the third time sins we left England. On the 18th Holey Stone all Decks and Exercise All day with Sails. On the 21st Morning wash Cloase and Scrub Hammocks and at 11 o'clok A M the Turkish Admiral Cum on Board And we Beat to General Quarters And as He Was Leaving we Mand Yards and Salutid Him and after Salutid Our Consell. He was with the Turkisk Admiral. In the Evning we Had a Boate cum Along Side of our Ship a Loaded as Hevvy as Poss-bill with soft Bread & potates and & Aiggs. On the 22nd A Verey fine Morning and the Pasha sent off to Us 6 Boolicks and 30 Sheep.

On the 23rd A fine Morning Aire Bedding. And thear was a Man Fell over Board but he was Picked Up All most as soon as He was in the Water. He was not Hurted. At 6 P M we waid Anchor and Maide Sail and Stood Out to sea. On the 24th Morning we Bout Ship and got Opasite Alexander But we Did Not Drop Anchor thear. We should A stowd and went into Alexandria Harbour on the 23rd But the wind was too strong for us to go over the Bar. There was a verey hevvy swell. General Quarters. On the 25th A Verey fine Morning Holey Stone All Decks. We past By Boka (Aboukir)Bay. Very Light wind at 11 P M. Lightning and thunder But No Rain But Blowing Rather Stiff. On the 26th No Divine Servis. In a Ded Calme All Day. On the 27th we was Coate by a Squall Thunder and Lightning and Rain . Very Much. At One o clok we came to our Anchoridge Oposite Alexander and then Dropt Anchor and Furled Sail. On the 28th Scrub and wash Cloase and Verey Fine to Dry them . In the Afternoon the Governer Of Alexander sent us 6 Bullocks and sum sheep and fowells and turkeys and potatoes and Aiggs and Many a Hundred Loves of Bread and Oranges and Lemons. Very fine All Day but Lightning at Night. On the 29th Watering Ship and shifting Jib Boom and Tagalant [2] Mast for Excersise. Lightning at Night. On the 30th Watering Ship and Excersise with Sails, Lightning at Night. On the 31st Morning Scrub and Washing Cloase – fine all Day. General Quarters in the fornoon and Again about 11 Oclok At Night.

On the First of November Holey Stone all Decks, fine all day. On the 2nd A fine Morning . No Divine Servis for the Chaplan was on Leff. Fine all Day. On the 3rd A Very Fine Day. Excersise with tagalant and topsail yards . On the 4th Morning Verey Fine. Scrub Hammocks and wash Cloase. On the 5th Very Hot. Excersise with sails and yards. On the 6th very Hot. air Bedding and Make and Mend Cloase. In the Evning shift the jibs in 3 Minits and Hallf. On the 7th Scrub and wash Cloase . General Quarters. In the fornoon A firing shot and shell at target. And we Had a Man fall Over Board But He Saved Him Self By taking Hold of a rope End. Verey Hot All Day. On the 8th Holey stone All decks. Fine All Day. *The Incounter* steamer Cum Out Of Alexander Harbour about 4 Oclok P M and at Hallf Past 6 Oclok we Waid Anchor. (November 8th 1851) And Maid sail and we Had A Good Breeze. We Left Alexander Very Well and we Had Very Good treatment thear for we Have Had one or two Cases Of Brain fever Sinas we Have Been Lying Hear But All Well at Preasent. On the 9th a Light Breeze. We had Divine Servis in the fornoon . Fine All Day. On the 10 & 11th Hot But not so much As it was at Alexander. In the evning of the 11th A Verey Strong Breeze. We was going from 11 to 12 knots Per Hour. On the 12th Not So Much Wind but Fine Wether. On the 13th Make and Mend Cloase. A good Breeze all days. On the 14th we cum to our Morings in Malta Harbour at 10 Oclok A M and as soon as we was in Harbour we was Put in Quarantine for 3 Days[3]. In the afternoon We un Bent sails and Lowerd our Lower Yards. On the 15th settin up the riggin. In the Evning send up the yards. On the 16th Holey stone Decks. In the fornoon Divine Servis. Lightning at night. On the 17th ree fitting the riggin. Thunder and Lightning and rain Verrey Hevvy In the Evning.

November 18th Ree fitting the riggin and watering Ship and getting in sum pervishons and Coaling Ship. Fine all day But a Light Rain at Night. On the 19th re fitting the riggen. We hav sum Corkers (caulkers) Cum on Board to day to Cork the Main and Lower Decks. A Littell rain at Night. On the 20th A Verey fine Morning and Admiral Parker and His Fleet Cum into This Harbour and we am Under His Command Now. The Fleet Hav Been Out on a Cruze for 2 or 3 months. In this Harbour now thear is *The queen* , *trafalger*, 3 Deckers, *Ganges, Suparbe* , *Albion and Vengeance* 2 Deckers and *the Turrabil* steamer. Today the Corkers Hav finished the Decks And we hav stowed away the Pervishons and A Cleaning Ship. On the 21st Fine but a Great Deal Colder than it was at Alexander. In the Afternoon the Port watch got 48 Hours Liff to go On Shoar. *The Belerophon* Cum into Harbour today and *the Erclus* (Hercules)on the 22nd. A fine Morning . We sent a Sailor Ashoar to Day and Gave Him His Discharge But He was soon In Jail for thieft. On the 23rd a fine day in the fornoon . Divine Servis. Rain in the Evning. Fine wether up to the 24th and on the 25th Starboard Watch went on Liff for 48 Hours and I went then. Fine wether up to 10th of December.

On the 11th we Had a Officer fall from the Mizzen Top[4] down to the Poop. He was sent to the Hospatell Direckly, Now we am with the Admiral the ruten is on Mundays , Shift jib Booms a tagalant Mast and on Thursdays bend on and bind sails and sum times Man and Arm Boats in the Afternoon. On Wednesdays all the Marines Do go on Shoar to Drill in Harbour ruteen.On Thursdays make and mend Cloase and Aire Bedding. On Fridays General Quarters an the fornoon and Man and Arm Boats in the afternoon. On Saturdays Holey Stone All Decks. On Sundays Clean guns. Go to Divitions. Divine Servis after. Fine up to the 17th of December. All Marines on Shoar to Drill. Fine wether But Rather Cold at Nights. But now it is as Hot Hear as ever I new it in Portsmouth Harbour in the Middell of Summer. On the 18th Excersise with Spars and Sails. On the 19th General Quarters in the Fornoon . Excersise with Spars.

In the Afternoon on the 20th a Littell rain. Holey Stone All Decks. On the 21st Divine Servis. In the Fornoon a Littell Rain In the Afternoon Rather Cold By Night But It Don't Seem Much Lick Crismas Wether To Me. On the 22nd All the Fleet Exersise with Spars and Sails. On the 23rd morning Scrub and Wash Cloase and Scrub Hammocks. A Littell rain in the fornoon But fine in the afternoon. The Sailors Went On Shoar to Drill With the Field Pisses and We Marines at Drill on Board. In the Evning We Had Orders to Land Next Morning at 7 Oclok All the Marines to Fire 20 rounds of Blank Catridges Each Man. On the 24th Wet Morning and Rain all day at times and that Prevented Us from going On Shoar to Drill. Lightning at Night. On the 25th Crismas Day. Very Fine. Divine Servis in the fornoon. This Day is Kept as

Sunday in the Navy. In the evning at Sunset as we was Sending Down the tagalant and royal yards there was a Man fell from the Main top and he pichud in the Main Chains. He was took in to the Sick Bay. He was in the List about 3 weeks. On the 26th General Quarters In the Fornoon . A Verey Hevvy Hail Storm In the afternoon . On the 27 Holey Stone all Decks . On the 28 Divine Servis In the Fornoon. We find it Very Cold Now. On the 29 and 30 and 31st Very Fine. On the Last of the Month All the Marines and Marine Artilary from all the fleet Landed and we was all Uni-form and we fired blank cartridges   And went throw a field Day and the Admiral was thear. Thear was between 11 and 12 hundred of Us[5].

On the First of January 1852 fine Wether and a Greate deel Warmer. Then it was fine up to the 5th and then it was rather Windy an Rain Verey Much all the for-noon And All the Ships in Harbour Did Send Down royal and tugalant yards and tagalaht Masts and Strick Lower yards and Topmast. On the 6th A Verey Fine Day and we send it All Up Again. Scrub Hammocks and Wash Cloase. On the 7th thear was a Sailor floged. He had 24 Lashes But His Sentence was 36 Lashes But As He Made So Much Noise the Captain forgave Him One Dozen. That was the first sailor That Has Been Floged sines I hav Bean Hear In This Ship and he is the only Man that has Cried Out while Receiving His Punishment sines I Have Bean In The Ship[6]. He Got it for Being Drunck and Noisey". On the 8th A Verey fine Day. All Marines Went On Shoar to Drill. On the 9th fine all day. On the 11th *the Queen Albion* and *Suparbe* Had Orders to Perpare for Sea and *the Albion* and *Suparbe* Bent Sails the same Day. On the 11th Verey Fine. Divine Servis. *The Queen* Bent Her Sails. On the 12th the Admiral Shifted His Flag from *the Queen* to Our Ship *The queen* and *the Albion* and *Suparbe* and the *Indefatigabill* Sailed Out Of This Harbour in the Morn-ing and in the First Watch they had General Quarters just Befor 12 Oclok P M. We Could Hire the Reports of Thear Guns.

On the 13th fine all Day and thear was a turkish Steam friget Went Out of this Har-bour to Day. In this Harbour Now there Is the trafalger *the Bellerophon* and Us and a Dutch Friget and a fuw small Steamers. On the 14th that Officer that fell from the Mizen Top to the Poop on the 11th of December Cum out from the Hospatell all Right But He Looks rather Peal. Fine wether up to the 18th. Divine Servis in the fornoon. Fine wether up to the 23rd. General Quarters in the fornoon. In the afternoon Clearing Up Decks for a Ball As We thought But Just Befor 2 Oclok P M the Admiral made a signal (January the 23rd 1852) for us and *the trafalger* and *the Bellerophon* to Preaper for Sea and that afternoon and Evning we Bent Sails Short-ened in Cable. On the Morning of the 26th the Admiral Shifted His flag from our Ship to *the turabul* and then We Got Up our Anchor And Made Sail an Stood Out to Sea for to join *the queen Albion* and *Suparbe*. And the Next Morning the 25th we Sited them At Day Breake and we got in Company with them in the fornoon.

The Queen and *trafalger* is 3 Deckers. Us and *the Bellerophon* and *Albion* and *Suparbe* is two deckers. *The Indefatigable* fregat is gon to Corfu. *The Queen* Left Us and went in to Harbour. On the 26th fine up to the 29thand all of us tried the Rate of Sailing And We Had a Good Breeze forit and Our Ship was the Second Best that Day [7]. On the 30th we all tried the rate of sailing Again and *the Suparbe* and Us Did Keep A Breast Of Each Other Kor Many A Mile. We and *the Suparbe* Left all the rest of them Many A Mile Behind Of Us. On the 31st the Breeze freshoned. The Senior Captain Made A Signal for us all to. Man and Arm Boats at one Oclok. And the Breeze Still Kept freshoning. And in the Evning We took in All Sails Excrpt the topsails and thay we reeft. It was My first Watch on Deck. I went on Duty at the Wheal at at 11 Oclok P M and then it was Blowing Very Hevvy And Just Befor 11 oclok P M She gave one or two Very Hevvy Lurches Over to Leeward and the Wheal took Charge and flung us all 4 from Her and the Wheal Broak One of the Mens Arms and Struck one or two more of Us But Not To Hurt Much [8]. It was Blowing a strong Gale All Night.

And on Sunday Morning the first of February it was Still incressing And in the fornoon we furald the topsails and Lowered the tagalant Mast and Yards on Deck and we set the storm Stasells And Then It Was Blowing A Verey Hevvy Gale And In the Evning It Was Blowing A Hurican. About Hallf Past 4 Oclok P M She Gave A Verey Hevvy Lurch and then She Pitched One of her Bigg Guns from of the for Castell Over Board. The gun was a 32 Pounder 2 tun 5 Hundred Waight. And we Lost One of Our Swinging Booms and 2 or 3 Studing Sail Booms Over Board. And it Was Blowing and Raining Verey Hard At Night. On the Morning of the 2nd we Caried away Her Main top sail And Had soon got it in ribons. We Caried Storm stunsls All that Day and Night. On the 3rd the Wind Beated a littell And We Bent A Nother Main topsail And set topsails And took in the Storm stasell And then We Made Our Best Way for Malta. We was Crusing off Malta and Scisley the time the Gale Cum On but as we Could Not Carry Any Sails We Drifted to Loward A great Many Miles. It was A Nor East Wind At the time of the gale. On the 4 5 and 6th a Strong Breeze But a Fowell Wind soe Never Sited any of the Other Ships After the Gale Cum On Untill we got to Malta on the 8th. A fine Morning. *The Trafalger Albion* and *Suparbe* Was in Harbour. Sum of them was in for 2 or 3 Days. *The trafalger* She went in About a Hallf a Hour Befor Us. *The trafalger* and *Bellerophon* recived More Damige tha Any of Us. We Comensed re fitting Ship To Day on the 9th. A verey fine Day. Divine Servis in the fornoon. Fine up to the 20th and then Corking and Painting Ship. Pay Money to Day. On the 21st *the Suparbe* Saild Out Of Malta Harbour for England to Be Paid Off. On the 22nd Wet and Windy. Divine Servis in the fornoon and in the afternoon about 2 oclok The Admiral Cum On Board Our Ship and Inspect Our Decks. In the Evning *the Phaeton* friget Went Out of Harbour to go to Corfu to releve the Incounter steamer. She Has got Orders to join the Lisbon Squaderon. Fine up to the 27th. *The Incounter* Cum in to Harbour on the 28th. A fine Day. At 8 Oclok P M We Had Orders to Preaper For Sea.

On the 1st of March We Bent Sails and got in some Water and Pervishons And we Let go of our Morings at 6 oclok Bell And Saild Out Of Harbour And Stood Out to Sea and *the turabel* steamer was with Us. On the 2nd a Strong Breeze But a fowell Wind for Us. In the evning we Made a Signal for *the turabel* to Make Her Best Way to the rock of Gibralter. On the 3rd and 4th a Strong Breeze Verey Cold Winds. On the 5th we Lost all the wind in a Ded Calme. In the first and Middell Watches Scrub and Wash Cloase. General Quarters to Day. Befor We Left Malta thear Was 3 Lieutenants Left Our Ship And there was 3 More joind in Thair Playsis. Them Went to England that Left Us. We left 1 Marine and 2 sailors Behind Us At Malta When we Saild They was Breaking thair Leff at the time. On the 6th A Little Breeze Sprung Up fair for us. On the 7th and 8th A good Strong Breeze and a fair Wind. We am going from 11 to 12 Knots the Wind not Hardly So Strong from 9 to 10 Knots Per Hour. On the 10th Very Light Wind. On the 11th in a Ded Calme Scrub and I Wash Cloase. On the 12th in a Ded Calme in the fornoon and we had General Quarters. A firing Shot in the Afternoon. The Breeze Sprung Up A Littell. On the 13th We run in to Harbour at the rock and as we run to Ny the Land we got A Ground [9] About One Bell after 8 oclok A M. We Squared Yards and Rold the Ship but Could Not Get Her Off. And then we Started more than A Hundred tons of her Fresh Water and transported Her Guns from the Forpart Of Her Decks to the After Part and Dropt two Cadge Anchors a Fuw Yards from Her Stem and by March 13th 1852 Heving with the Captson and Roling the Ship We Got Her Off By 7 Oclok P M and then we Dropt Anchor for that Night And Piped to Super and Splist the Main Brase. Keep Anchor Watch All Night. On the 14th Sunday we got Her to Her Proper Anchoridge and Mored Her. Thear was the turibul and *Incounter* and *jeaniss (Genius?)* steamers thear in Harbour. Verey Hevvy rain and Wind .

On the 15th We Sent off two Boats Ashoar after Water but the wind was too strong for them to Bring any Off to the Ship. *The Albion* Past by hear to day for Lisbon and Had a good Breeze through the Gut. On the 16th Wash and Scrub Cloase. At 8 Oclok send up tagalant yards and Mast and Loose Sails. Fine Morning Watering Ship. We has got in Between 2 and 3 Hundred tons. We do Carry Four Hundred and 64 tons when we am fild up. On the 18th a Wet Morning. Hands Make and Mend Cloase. On the 19th wash and scrub Cloase. We sent Up Tagalant Mast and yards and Loost Sails. General Quarters. In the fornoon furald sails and

Shipped topsail Yards. In the afternoon on the 20th Holey Stone All Decks And A Verey fine Day. March 21st A Strong Breeze. Divine Servis in the fornoon. On the 22nd A Very Strong Breeze. Sent down the tagalant Mast and yards. Exercisin with the Lower Deck Quarters. On the 23rd Scrub Hammocks and wash Cloase. But We Could Not Dry them that Day. Main Deck quarters in the fornoon. A Strong Breeze All Day. On the 24th A Fine Morning and Not So Much wind. We sent up the tagalant Masts and the tagalant and royal yards and Hung up the Hammocks. After Quarters and Exercisin with Spars. On the 25th settin up the riggin and taking in what water and Pervishons and Coals we wants. A weet day.

On the 27th Holey Stone All Decks. Stormey all day. On the 28th Divine Servis in the fornoon and in the afternoon gave Leff. Stormey at times all dayOn the 29th a Strong wind Loos sails at 8 o clok. Furld them Befor Dinertime. On the 30th and 31st fine wether send up tagalant Mast and Loos sails. Furl them at 7 Bells in the fornoon. Send Down Mast and yards at Sunset . On the first of April a fine day Painting Ship. The watch Below Make and Mend. (April 1st 1852) Cloase on the 2nd fine all day. *The Queen* Cum in Hear to this Harbour About 3 o clok P M. Admiral Parker was On Board *the Queen*. We saluted the governor with 17 guns. And then Dropt Anchor. Scrub and Wash Cloase. This morning *the Erclus* Cum in Harbour About 6 Bells in the First Watch. Painting Ship today. On the 3rd very Fine . Painting Ship. On the 4th a fine day. Divine Servis. On the 5th Lower Deck Excersise rain at times. On the 6th Scrub Hammocks and Wash Cloase. A Fine Day to Day. Then *the Erclus* was towed Out of Harbour By *the Spitfull* steamer. On the 7th Morning the Steamer took *the Queen* in Tow and took her throw the gut and then She Had Got A fair wind for England. As She was Leaving We Cheered Her. Fine All Day. On the 8th fine wether sent up the tagalant and royal yards and Loos Sails. Sent them Down At Sunset. On the 9th fine wether Divine Servis. It is Good Friday. It is keept as Sunday. On the 10th fine All day. Holey Stone All Decks. On the 12th a fine morning . Send up yards and Loose Sails. In the fornoon thear was A Man Died On Board Our Ship on Good Friday and he was Buried on Sunday the 11th. Scrub and Wash Cloase weet all day.

On the 14th fine all day. Send up yards and Loos sails Shift jib Boom and tagalant Mast. Fine up to the 16th General Quarters in the Afternoon. I Went on Shoar on Leff for 24 Hours And I Stopt For 60 More [10]. Fine up to the 22nd. That day there was 3 Sailors flogged for Being Drunck on Duty two of them and the other for thieft. Fine up to the 25th . Divine Servis. In the fornoon *the Albion* and *the Indefatigable* frigget Cum in this Harbour. The Captain of *the Albion* is Senior to Our Captain and now we am Under His Controll. Fine up to the 29th. To day thear was Me and A Nother Man Lost Our Good Conduct Badges For 12 Months And 2 Petty

Officers Disraeted. Fine up to the 5th of May then us and *Albion* and *Indefategable* and *turabel* Waid Anchor and maid sail and stood Out to sea with a Light Breeze. On the 7th thear was a Corproal of Marines Loast One of His Strips for Cumin Off to the Ship Drunk And a Blue Jacket Lost One For Bringing Spirats In to the Ship. Fine up to the 9th.

The Phaeton joind us on the 10th. We flogged a Marine. He had 30 Lashes for Stricking A Lance Corpoarl. At 6 P M we fell in with the Admiral and His Squadron. Thear is two three Deckers and three two Deckers two frigets and two Steamers. Fine up to the 15th. A Light Breeze. We Has Had A Very Light Wind Ever Sines We Had Beain From the Rock. About 4 oclok P M we was towed in to Portmahon Harbour Spain. And Dropt anchor and furld sails. On the 16th the Admiral made a Signal for Divine Servis in the fornoon and for One Hundred Men to go On Shoar for 24 Hours Leff from all the Liners and 50 Each of the friggets and Steamers. On the 17th A Very fine Day. *The Indefategable* and a Steamer got on the Way and stood out to Sea. Watering Ship for this last two Days. We Comenst waring White trousers on the 16th of May. Very fine up to the 23rd of May. Divine Servis in the Fornoon. At Sunset in the Evning after Sending down the yards as the Men was Cuming Down from Aloft One Man fell From the for top over board. He was not Kild. It was Our Majesties Birthday. We sent up tagalant yards and Drest Ship at 8 oclok A M and at 12 oclok we Mand yards and Fired a royal Salute and Gave Three Cheers send down yards and On Drest Ship. On the 25th send up tagalant and royal yards and the Admiral Cum on Board Our Ship And We Beat To General Quarters And After Quarters the Admiral Inspected the Ships Company and He was Verey Much Pleased By Our Drill. On the 26th the Collinell of Marines Cum on Board from the flag Ship and Inspected Us Marines. On the 27th and 28th Open Ship. On the 29th Clean All Decks. On the 31st Verey fine. Divine Servis in the fornoon. Preapering for sea.

On the 1st of June We all waid anchor and stood out to Sea. We was Out Of Harbour by 8 A M. About 10 in the first (watch?) We was Coat in a Squall. It did thunder and Lightning and Rain Verey Hevvy. On the 2nd We had a Strong Breeze and We All Tried the rate of sailing and We did Beate All Of them Excepting *the Phaeton* friget. Verey Fine up to the 6th Morning thear was A Boy fell from the Main Lower Riggen. In the fornoon Divine Servis. Fine Wether up to the 9th. All Of Us Had General Quarters at Hallf Past 3 oclok A M. Hot Fire. Fine the 10th and 11th General Quarters on the 11. (June the 12th 1852) Holey Stone All Decks. On the 13th Divine Servis. On the 14th and 15th In a ded Calme. On the 16th A Verey Strong Breeze In the Evning We Carried Away Our for top Sail and for Stasel In the first watch We Carried Away Our Main Sail. Afterwards we was Under Cloas reef topsails. On the 17th A Strong Breeze On the 18th Not So Much Wind. Qeneral Quarters. A Hevvy Swell. After Quarters A Man fell Over Board But Was Soon Picked Up All Right. On the 19th Verey Light Wind. On the 20th In a ded Calme.

In the fornoon thear was A Man took in a Fit And In A Hallf A Hour He Was Ded. On the 22nd that Man was Buried at Sea. On the 23rd a Strong Breeze and we all tried the rate of Sailing and *the Phaeton* is the Only one that is with us that Can Keep Up With Us. All of us Dropt anchor at 5 Oclok P M just off the Plains of Almeria Spain. On the 24th Befor Breakfast we all waid Anchor and we had a Light Breeze But Soon Lost It Again and we Dropt Anchor the Same Day. On the 25th General Quarters A firing at targets. On the 26th fine wether. On the 27th A Light Breeze. Divine Servis. On the 28th Foggey but a Littel Wind . We got in Harbour at the rock And Dropt Anchor At About 7 Bells in the first Watch. All of us Except Belerophon Did Not Cum in untill Sum time in the Middel watch. *The trafalger* Did Not Cum In Befor Next Morning. On the 29th A Fine Day. Mored Ship Got Out All Boats On Bent All Small Sails. On the 30th A fine Morning. Up tagalant yards and Loos Sails. Fural sails at 6 Bells.

On the 1st and 2nd of July Watering and Pervishoning Ship. On the 3rd All Marines and Marine Artilleary from All the Ships Landed A Shoar at the rock at 6 A M to Drill. In the Afternoon Pay Money to the Ships Company. Watering Ship. On the 4th sent up yards at 8 AM In the fornoon Divine Servis. Fine all day. On the 5th the Small Arm Blue Jackets Landed Ashoar to Drill. Watering Ship and getting in sum Pervishons. On the 6th Fine Morning and We All Had Orders Preaper for sea and We All Bent Small sails . On the 7th A Verey Fine Morning. We got on what Water and Pervishons we wanted in the fornoon. In the Afternoon We Got In all Boats and Shorten in Cabel. At 6 P M We Waid Anchor. The Bratania flag and *trafalgar* 3 Deckers *Vengeance* and *Bellerophon* and *Albion* 2 Deckers 2 frigets 2 steamers . One of the steamers took *the trafalger* in tow Out Side. On the 8th Verey fine all day .General Quarters in the fornoon. In the Afternoon Aire Bedding. At night Scrub and wash Cloase. On the 9th A Very fine Morning Bathing at sea. On the 10th a fine morning But A Light Breeze. Holey Stone All Decks . And We Sailed Very Close to Maluga. On the 11th A Very Light Breeze Divine Servis in the fornoon. On the 12th Very Fine all Day.

On the 13th Very Fine. The Admiral Sent Us 4 Bullocks that is 2 days fresh meat for Us [11] and all the fleet Had Sum. We am Crusing Off Malaga still. On the 14th Verey Hot. In a ded Calme We Hav Excersise With Spars or Sails Most Evry Evning On the 15th Verey Hot. General Quarters in the fornoon. Air Bedding in the Afternoon. Exercise with sails after supper. To Day there was 4 steamers joind us 2

Steam friggets and two smaller ones Just Cum Out of England. This morning at 4 oclok A M beat to General Quarters and a gain at 7 o clok AM. A firing at targets at 9 oclok . On the 16th Very Hot. Divine Servis. Shifting Jib in the fornoon . Bathing in the Evning. In a ded Calme then on the 17th A Strong Breeze tried the rate of sailing all of us. We was 2nd Ship runing with the wind And 5 Ship runing(?)Against the wind. We caried away our Jib and that throwed us behind.July 18th In A Ded Calme . Verey Hot. Divine Servis.

On the 19th A Light Breeze. All of us tried the rate of sailing. Set Studding sails and Sails Lower and A Loaft then we Beat all the fleet. In the Evning We all Had Orders to Shift topsails and Corses. We Dun it Complate in 6 Minits and 40 secinds that was 2 minits befor Any Other Ship in the Fleet. On the 20th morning Scrub Hammocks and wash Cloase. In the fornoon the Admiral maed a Signal for All of Us to Shift topsail yards. *The Phaeton* friget was first at that. She was 16 minits and 40 secunds And us was 17 minits and 15 secunds. We was 2nd Ship at that. On the 21st Verey fine all day. On the 22nd General Quarters at 4 A M And at 9 A M riff topsails. And we kild two Bullocks. In the evning Scrub and Wash clean. In the First and Middell Watches on the 23rd Very Fine . All of us at Ball Practes The Marines and Small Arm Men. At Evning Verey Foggy In the Middell watch We Had A Boy fell from the Mizen top and Struck against a Boat and was kild.

On the 24th A Light Breeze Very Hot. In the Evning fural sails and Shift tagalant Mast. The two frigets was Befor Us But all the rest of them was Behind us. July 25thA Light Breeze. Divine Servis in the fornoon. After Servis we Buried that Boy not far from where we buried that other Man. We just off Cape Cadet now off the Spanish Land. On the 26th Verey Hot all day. Riff topsails at Evning Fural wash Cloase at night. On the 27th Verey Hot All Day. Exersisin With Sails at Evning fural and loos and maek sail .On the 28th Verey Hot All day. In the Evning fural sails and maek sail and set all Studding sails Lower and A Loaft. On the 29th In A Ded Calme general Quarters In the fornoon. A Firing Shot and Shell In the Evning. The Breeze Freshoned at Night. Wash Cloase. On the 30th A Good Breeze. We had a Sailing Match. On the 31st Nearly in a Ded Calme. Holey Stone All Decks to Day. We had 4 Bullocks sent to us and we Kild 2 of them after Quarters. In the Evning Pipe Hands to Bath.

On the 1st of August Pipe Hands to Bath In the Morning in a Ded Calme. Divine Servis in the fornoon. We had a Littell Wind in the Evning . On the 2nd a Strong Breeze in the fornoon. We tried the rate of Sailing we was the second Ship at that. At Evning we Shifted topsails and Courses. *The Indefatigable* and us was 10 minits and 30 seconds and All Of the Rest Was A Great Deal More. August 3rd A Strong

Breeze all day. On the foarth Trying the Rate of Sailing By Day and at Evning Exersise With Sails. On the 5th A Strong Breeze and we Had Orders to Make Our Best Way to the rock and then We Soon Parted Company with the fleet. We had topsails and 6th A Good Breeze and we got in Harbour at the Rock and Dropt Anchor. At 5 Oclok Bell fural sails and Squard yards and Courses set at the time and 3 reffs in our topsails. Wash Cloase at night. On the Got Out All Boats. On the 7th Holey Stone All Decks in the morning. In the afternoon Shift tagalant Masts and fural sails and setting up the Top mast riggen and Blackening Down the riggen. On the 8th Very Fine. Divine Servis. On the 9th Verey Fine All Day. On the 10th fine wether. All the Marines Landed from all the Shipping And Was Inspected By the Admiral and the Govener of Gibralter and they was Very Much Pleased By Our Studeeness in the Rainks. Afterwards went on Shoar On Leff. On the 11th the Small Arm Blu Jackets Went On Shoar to Drill with the field Pisses. Afterwards they went on Shoar on Leff. Today the Steamers that Joind us.

On the 15th of July Left This Harbour for England and our sergeant Maijor was invalided and He Went Home In One Of The Steamers. Verey fine up to the 15th. Watering and Pervishoning Ship. In the morning Divine Servis in the fornoon. In the Evning Got In All Boats and Bent On All Small Sails. On the 16th We On Mored Ship and Shorten in Cabel in the fornoon and in the Afternoon we waid Anchor and Maid Sail but we was forst to fural Sails and there was A Steamer took Us in tow. On the 17th A Light Breeze. On the 18th A Good Breeze and a fair Wind. Set Studding Sails Lower and A Loaft. On the 19th a fowell wind. General Quarters in the fornoon. A Fair Wind in the Evning. Scrub and Wash Cloase. On the 20th A Fine Morning .In the fornoon Shift Fortopsail. First Ship at that. On the 21st a Light Breeze but fowell. At Evning Shift topsails and Courses in 7 minits and we was the First Ship in the fleet. On the 22nd A Verey fine Day. Divine Servis in the fornoon. A Strong Breeze All Day and we spliit the Jib in the Middell watch.

On the 23rd A fine Day and a Light Breeze. The Small Arm Blu Jackets annd BoatScrows was at Ball Practes. Scrub and wash Cloase at Night . On the 24th A Strong Breeze in the forpart of the Day In the evning In All Most A Ded CaLme. On the 25th Verey fine and Hot. A Light Breeze. When we left the rock on the 16th of this month We Left Behind Us Belonging to this Ship 5 Marines and 8 Sailors A Breaking Thear Liberty. On the 26th general Quarters. A Firing Shot or Shull. On the 27th A Strong Breeze but Fowell for Malta. On the 28th a Light Breeze on the 29th A Fine day. Divine Servis in the fornoon. On the 30th We Hove to and Spoke to a Murchant Vessel And Asked Her if Any of the french Fleet was at Malta and Her Answer Was No. Scrub Hammocks and Wash Cloase at Night. On the 31st A Light Breeze in the Afternoon. The Captain of the Ship and the Captain of Marines Went

On Board the Flag Ship and Dined With the Admiral. Lightning at Night.

September the 1st 1852 In A ded Calme. In the Morning A Breeze Sprung Up about 10 Oclok A M. We set Studding Sails Lower and A Loaft After Super Shipt Maintop-sail and reef topsails in 2 minits and 40 seconds. At 12 Oclok Mid Night We Past By Whear *the Venger* [12] was Lost in 1848. It is About 190 Miles from Malta. On the 2nd General Quarters In the Fornoon. Air Bedding in the Afternoon And thear was A Boy Fell Over Bord from the riggen . The Life Boy was Let Go And He Took Hold of Him and Saved Him Sellf. We was going throu the Water then About 8 knots Per Hour. Lightning at Night. Scrub and wash Cloase. On the 3rd A Light Breeze and fair for Malta. Studding Sails set Lower and A Loaft. Make and Mend Cloase. Light-ning at Night. On the 4th We Sited Malta at Day Break. We got Opasite Malta at Breakfast time and we Lay to All Day. Our Comander Cum Back Of 10 day Leff. We got in what they wanted in the Ward room and Gun room. In the evning we Bracd Up and Stood Out to Sea. In A ded Calme . Lightning at Night. On the 5th A fine Morning But No Wind. Divine Servis in the Fornoon. And We Took in A Pilat in the Afternoon. On the 6th A Light Wind. All day Very Hot. Lightning at Night. On the 7th Verey Light Wind A Little Rain in the Evning. On the 8th in A ded Calme in the For Part of the day. Piped hands to Bath. In the Evning after Super Shipt topsails and Courses in 5 Minits and 30 seconds And we was By Far the First Ship. In a ded Calme . Lightning Very Much in the first watch.

When we Left Malta *the turabel* steamer and *Incounter* friget Parted Company from Us. They Had Orders for England to Be Paid Off. On the 9th A Very Light Wind. General Quarters. In the for Noon A firing at targets. Wash Cloase At Night And in a ded Calm all Night. On the 10th A fine Morning And Very Hot . All Most in a ded Calm all day. On the 9th *the tiger* Steamer Joind Us. She was just Cum from England. On the 11th Very Hot All Day. *The Albion* was Put in Quaruntine for 3 Days for Bording a Murchant Ship to day. On the 12th A ded Calm in the fornoon. Divine Servis in the fornoon. In the Afternoon A Light Breeze. On the 13th A Good Breeze reef topsails after Super. September 14th A Very Light Breeze. In the Evning the *tiger* took *the trafalger* and *Bellerophon* In tow and the *firebrand* took the *Bratania* And *Albion* In Tow. Us and *the Phaeton* was Left Behind to Make the Best Of Our Way to Vola Bay. On thr 15th A Very Light Breeze. At Dinnertime We Had Lime Dues Servd Out to Us for the first time. On the 15th A Strong Breeze All Day. General Quarters in the fornoon. On the 17th A Light Breeze all day. In a ded calm. At Night Pipe Hands to Lower Deck Quarters And at 12 Oclok the turkish Bathe.

We Had Lime Dues today. On the 18th in a ded Calm untill the Evning and then We Had A Littell Breeze. On the 19th A good Strong Breeze and we was forsd to reef topsails and we Caried Away Our Fortopsail And Was forst to Bend Another in Its Plase. It Was Only A Land Breeze. In A Hallf A Hour afterward We was in a Ded Calm. We was Going Between A Greate Many Islands at the Time. *The Phaeton* was Not far From Us. We got in to Voulrah Bay about 2 Bells in the afternoon watch And Dropt Anchor and furald Sails and Squared yards and Mored Ship and then Pipe to diner. After Diner Serve Out Lime Dues. Fine all day. No Divine Servis to day. September 20thA Good Breeze. ree stowing Booms and Blackening Down the riggen. We gave Leff to the Officers Only. Fresh Meat today. We have bean 34 days On Salt Meat [13]. In this Bay now thear is *the Bratania* Flag Ship *Admiral Dundass* and *the trafalger* 3 decker and *Albion* and *Vengeance* and *Bellerophon* 2 deckers and *the Phaeton* friget and *the tiger* Steamer. The Admiral have sent *the firebrand* steamer to Malta with Our Mail for England. The turkish shippng in this Harbour is one Dubell Baink friget Caries A Admiral and two frigets and One Brigg And A Brigateen and a Small Steamer. On the 21st a fine day Watering Ship. At 6 P M Our Admiral and All Of Our Post Captains and Commanders Went On Board Of the Dubell Banck frigget And Dined With the turkish Admiral[14] And thear was a french Steamer Cum in to this Bay this Evning and went round All of us and then Stood out to Sea Again. Watering Ship Alll Night.

On the 22nd A fine Day watering ship. We finished in the afternoon. Painting Ship Now. On the 23rd the Admiral went On Board *the trafalger* And On Board *the Trafalger* they Mand Yards and Saluted Him With 17 Guns and after He Left that Ship He Cum On Board Of Our Ship And we Mand yards and Saluted Him When He Cum On Board And As He was Leaving . After He Left Our Ship He Went On Board *the Bellerophon* And All Of Our Ships and He Inspected All Of the Ships Companys. The fresh Meate Hear was Better than it is at the rock of Gibralter. This Bay is about 7 Hundred miles from Malta Up the Arches A Pilego And it is 21 Miles from Hear to Smyrna. It is turkey in asia. On the 24th fine wether A Good Breeze. It is Much Colder Hear Than it is in Malta . Thear is Boates Rasing Hear Most Days. The admiral and Sum of His Officers went On Board our flag Ship and Most All of Our Post Captains And Dined With Our admiral And After they was all on Board the turks fired 2 royal salutes And So Did We And After it was Dark About 11 Oclok We Had Illumanation On Board Of All the Ships in Harbour and sent up rockets and Burnt Blu Lights. On the 25th A Strong Breeze. Man and Arm Boats in the fornoon. On the 26th A Good Breeze. Divine Servis in the Fornoon. On the 27th fine but a Good Breeze. September 28th A Verey fine Morning . Scrub Hammocks and wash Cloase. In the fornoon Bent All small Sails. In the afternoon We got All Our Boom Boats and in the Evning We Un Mored Ship and got Up One of Our anchors. On the 29th at 4 Oclok A M we turnd the Hands Up and Shortnd in the Cabel Of the Other anchor. About 8 Oclok A M We waid anchor and Maid Sail and Stood Out to Sea. The turkish Squadron Went Out About 2 Hours Befor Us . We Hav found this Plase More Helthier than Aney that We Have Bean in Latley. A Light Breeze When we Left the Bay But we Loast it All in the Evning. On the 30th. On the 30th Morning We Furuld Sails and the fuerey Steamer took Us and the *Phaeton* Frigit in tow about 8 A M .General Quarters in the Fornoon. In the Evning All of us Shifted topsail yards But Woork don't Go So Well On Board This Ship As It Hav Becose Our Commander is Sick.

October the 1st A Verey fine Day. The Steamers Let Go Of Us At 4 Oclok P M And we Dropt Our Best Bower anchor And Loost Sails and Squared yards. After Super fural sails. Our Commander Cum to His Duty To Day. He was sick for 10 days. *The Sampson* Steamer joind our Squadron this fornoon. She is from England . All the Captains Dined On Board *the Bratania* With the Admiral this Evning. This is a Much Warmer Plase Hear than it was at Voulrahy. This is Portandame Bay. It is about 40 Miles from Athens. We have Loast site of the turkish Squadron. As soon as we Dropt Anchor Hear in Portadama Bay the Admiral Put His Sellf and all the rest of us in Quarantine. On the 2nd A Verey fine Day. General Quarters in the fornoon A Firing Shot and Shell and Grape and Canusters at Targets. All the Shiping Bathing At Evning. Holey Stone the Lower Deck and Air Bedding In the Afternoon. On the 3rd At Hallf Past 4 Oclok A M We Turnd the Hands Up and Got Up Our Anchor And thear was a Steamsr took Us and *the Phaeton* In tow and towed us in to Sallmonds Bay and we Dropt Anchor at 6 P M and by 8 P M we was all in thear safe at Anchor. On Bent All small sails and Mored Ship. On the 4th We Got Out All Boats Befor Breakfast. In the afternoon we sent Home One Officer One Marine One Sailor And One Of the Band. Thay was not fit for Duty. The Captains All Dined On Board the admirals Ship this Evning. Fine all day. On the 5th Turn the Hands Up at 2 Oclok A M and Scrub and Wash Cloase until 5 Oclok A M. Shift jib Boom and tagalant Mast in 11 Minits and 30 secons. Afterwards the Admiral made a signal to Strike tagalant Mast and one Minit after for All Hands to Bathe. In the Afternoon Shift Mizen Topsail .

On the 6th Verey Dull But No rain. Fresh Meat To Day. We sent up tagalant Masts and Yards and loost Sails at 8 Oclok AM and furald sails at 10 AM . Bathing at Evning. On the 7th Verey fine all day and Hot. At 8 Oclok AM sent up tagalant yards and we Hoisted the Greekish Royal Standard and at 10 A M We All Fired a royal Salute. General Quarters in the fornoon. Send Down the tagalant yards and the Greekish Standard at Sunset. Leff for the Officers onley. The Admiral and Most all the Captains Hav Been on 3 or 4 Days Leff. On the 8th Verey fine all Day. In the for-noon one watch of Marines At Drill. In the afternoon Maek and Mend Cloase. The steamers Have Bean In to Athens Harbour to fell up with Coals. We am Lying Now in Sallmonds Bay but We Can See Athens Harbour Quit Plain. In the Evning We Shifted For and Main topsail yards . For in 13 Minits and Main in 16 Minits and 30 seconds.October 9th Holey Stone all Decks. In the Morning send up tagalant yards and Loos sails at 8 Oclok AM and Spreed all Morning. At 2 Oclok the french Admiral Cum On Board of Our Ship And Inspected the Ships Company And He So One or Two Guns Scrus Drill. As He Left the Ship We Saluted Him By 13 Guns. On the 10th fine all day . Divine Servis in the fornoon. In the Evning after super we got in our Boom Boats and Bent All Small Sail and got up misinger. On the 11th at 5 Oclok A M turn the Hands up And We Got Up our anchor And Shortend In the Cabel of the Other and then Pipe to Breakfast. And after Breakfast we got up the Other anchor and thear was a Steamer took us and *the Phaeton* in tow at 8 AM and all the Other Ships was took in tow By steamers.

We Left Salmonds Bay all Well. We got Another Marine Last Night in the Plase of that One that was Invalidid Home. Fine all Day. Scrub Hammocks and wash Cloase At Night. On the 12th A Verey Fine Day to Dry the Cloase and Hammocks. A Light Breeze all day Not So Hot As We Have Had It. We Lost all the wind in the afternoon and furd sails About 6 Bells in the afternoon and about 7 Bells A Steamer took us and *the trafalger* in tow and all the other ships was took in tow bur *the Phaeton* Frigget. Very Hot all Night. On the 14th A fine Morning and a Littell Breeze About 6 Bells in the Morning watch. October the 13th We Let Go of *the trafalger* And about 7 Bells the steamer Let Go of us and We Made Sail But A Light Wind. In the Evning In a Ded Calme. Shift topsails and Courses. On the 14th A fine Morning. About quarter to 4 Oclok We Had Qeneral Quarters. This Morning We found that sum Man or Men Had Cut 2 or 3 Of the Ropes about the Ship But We hav not found who it was that Dun it. General Quarters in the fornoon Air Bedding In the afternoon . Very light wind all day. Reef topsails in the Evning. Verey Muggey and Hot. We was just Opasite to Navarino [15] when we was at General Quarters. To Day wash Cloase at Night. On the 15th A fine Morning. In the fornoon Marines and small arm Blu Jackets was A firing at targets. Very light Breeze. Just Befor 5 Oclok P M While the Men was Going A Loaft thear was One Man fell through the Main riggen and he Pitchud on the Quarter Deck And He Hurt Him Sellf Very Much. He Died about A Hallf A Hour after He fell.

Reef topsails after Super. A Good Breeze At Night. On the 16th A Strong Breeze all day. All of the Ships A trying the rate of sailing and we was the first ship as *the Phaeton* was Parted Company from Us. About 4 Bells In the Afternoon We Buried that Man that Fell from the riggen. We was Opasite Zante at the time we Buried Him. reef topsails after. After Super Lightning. Very fast all Night. On the 17th Morning rain A Little. At 8 Oclok A M It Cleard Off Again And we went to Divisions In White as yousal. Divine Servis in the fornoon for the Watch Below But about 4 Bells It Did Look rather wild to Lowward and we took In Our studding sails and soon afterwards we shortend All Sail And took In 3 reefs in the topsails and Lowerd the topsail yards on the Caps and Hoist the for top mast staysel and By that time It Did thunder and Lightning and Rain Verey Hevvy But Not Verey Much Wind. It Lasted for About 3 Hours. About 6 Bells in the afternoon watch we Shook Out all reefs and Made Sail. In the first Dog watch It Was Verey Fine But Just Befor 6 Oclok P M It Did Look Verey Wild All Round Us and did Lightning. At 7 Oclok P M we turnd the Hands Up and shortnd all sail took in 3 reefs in the topsails and furald the for-sail and Lowerd the topsail yard on the Caps But soon after 8 Oclok we Hoist the topsails and set the Spankers and was runing all Night under that Sail. Lightning verey Strong all Night but Not Much Rain. On the 18th A fine Morning and A good Breeze We shook out all reefs and Maed Sail But thear was A Hevvy Swell. In the Evning we took in 3 reefs. Squaley All Night.

October 19th A Very fine Morning. A Light Breeze. In the afternoon we Lost all the Wind and furald sails about 7 Bells and *the tiger* steamer took us and *the Bellero-phon* and we On Bent all Small Sails and the steamer Let Go of us at 1 Bell after 6 in the Evning and after we Dropt Both anchors And Mored Ship In the Corfu Harbour. This Plase is about 5 Hundred Miles from Malta. It is the Capitall Of the Ionian Islands Whear Government Sits. On the 20th A Little rain in the morning. In the fornoon we got out all the Boom Boats. In the Afternoon We Let *the Arethusa* friget Have More than a Hundred Baggs of Breed and Sum Casks of salt Pervis-hons. She was going to stay thear for Sum time. Fine all day But Colder than we Hav found it sines last Winter. In this Harbour Now there is 5 Liners 2 friggets 1 Brigg and 7 steamers total 15. On the 21st fine Morning and we sent up the Galant yards at 8 Oclok AM watering ship afterwards. At 7 Bells in the afternoon Man and arm Boats and at Sunset send down tagalant yards and Disarm Boats. No General Quarters to Day On Acount Of Watering Ship.

On the 22nd A Fine Morning and all the Marines And Marine Artilleary Landed from All Our Ships and steamers at 9 Oclok A M and was Inspected By the Govern-er General and Admiral Dundass and afterwards we went throu a field day take In the Sail But we furald all sail as soon as Posabill. It did thunder and rain and Blow . We Did Muster About 11 Hundred Officers and Non commishon Officers and Men. We returnd to Our Ships about 7 Bells in the Fornoon. A Privat soldier belonging to the 30thrRegiment was Shot for stricking a Officer and thear was 7 or 8 transport-ed For Mutinous Conduct. On the Last of August 1852. On the 23rd A Fine day. Holey Stone and Clean All Decks and Black Down Riggen And got in sum Water. Up tagalant yards and Loos sails at 8 Oclok A M. At 6 Bells in the fornoon Fural Sails, and send down tagalant yards at Sunset. On the 24th A Verey fine Day and Verey Hot. Divine Servis in the fornoon. Bathing in the Evning. Last week the Purser Paid 3 Munths Mess Money to the Ships Company. On the 25th A Verey fine Morning and All the Small Arm Blu Jacket Men Landed from All the Shiping With thear Arms and field Pisses *(pieces)* and went throu a Field Day A firing off Blanck Catridges and thear was One Man Had His Arm Blowen Off while He Was Loading the field Piss. He did belong to *the Phaeton* frigget. About 6 Bells in the Afternoon we Loost sails. After Super fural Sails. October the 26thScrub Hammocks and wash Cloase in the Morning watch. Bent all Small Sails in the fornoon and we got in the Boom Boats in the Afternoon. After Super we went to Divitions with our Hammocks and returnd them afterwards. We beate to Quarters and secured the Guns for Sea Servis and got all things ready for onmoring Ship.

On the 27th A fine Morning. Turn the Hands Up At 4 Oclok and Unmored Ship and We Got Up One Anchor and Pipe to Breakfast. And about 3 Bells in the fornoon We got Up the Other Anchor And Loost and Maid Sail. A Light Breeze All Day. In the Afternoon the Admirals Ship and One or Two More furald sails and was took In tow By Steamers And They Was Towed Out Clear of the Land. We Laid About a Quarter Of A Mile from the town of Corfu . From the Entrens of the Harbour up to the town is 20 Miles Or More. In the Evning we took In What Studding Sails We Had Set But not Reeft Topsails. About 3 Bells In the first Watch we shortend and furald all sailsand *the Tiger* Steamer took Us In tow. Verey Light Wind and what thear was it was Fowell for Us. On the 28th About 1 Oclok A M the Steamer Let Go of us and we Made Sail. A Light Breeze. In the fornoon Shipt Main Topsail. In the afternoon A Stiff Breeze reef topsails after Super. On the 29th About 2 Oclok A M It Did thunder and Lightning Very Strong And It Did Look Very wild to windard . We shortnd all sail and furald the topsails But the Storm Past By us. We Made Sail Again the same Watch. In the fornoon we all Shifted fortopsails. We shifted ours in 6 Minits and 10 secunds. *The Bellerophon* was the Next Ship to Us She was 7 Minits and 30 secunds. Sum of the Ships was 15 Minits. It Was Blowing A Strong Breeze all day. We Had One Reff in the topsails all day and we took in 2 More In the Evning. It Did Look Verey Squaley at this time. In the first watch it did Lightning Verey Much. On the 30th A Light Breeze. The friggets Parted Company from Us About Mid day. *The arethusa* went to Corfu and *the Phaeton* went to Malta. In the Evning Fural and Loos and Make Sail. Verey Light Wind All Night. On the 31st A fine Morning. Divine Servis In the Fornoon for the watch Below. A Light Breeze All Day, Riff topsails In the Evning A Light Breeze All Day and a Fair Wind for Malta. Now at 6 P M we am just Opasite Mount Etney one of the firey Mountains. It is just 14 months to day that we left England.

On the 1st of November A fine Morning And all day A fair Wind for Malta. At Night in All Most a ded Calm. Wash Cloase. We took in One Reff in the topsails. On the 2nd a Verey fine Morning. A Light Wind. Set Studingsails Lower and A Loaft. At 4 Bells in the fornoon we Made Our Best Way for Malta as we thought But at 2 Oclok P M the Admiral Made A Signal for Us to shorten sail as we was going A Hed of Him. In the Evning In All Most A ded Calm At 3 Bells in the first Dog Watch thear was steamers took All of the Ships in tow Except Us and they got into Malta Harbour the Same Night. On the 3rd Morning at Day Breake We Sited Malta. At 6 Bells in the Morning Watch We run in to Malta Harbour and Made fast to a Buoy and then Pipe to Breakfast. Fural sails and then we got to our Morings and Mored Ship At 5 Bells in the fornoon And We Got Out the Boats and Loost Sails. After Diner we on bent all sails and Paid Money to One Watch and gave them 48 Hours Leff. We Hav But Verey Littell Wind.

November the 4th A Verey fine Morning and a Verey Hevy Du. Watering Ship after Breakfast and Clearing Out the Hoals and setting up the Riggen And returnin Old Stors And getting New in Plase of Others. On the 5th A fine Morning. After Breakfast getting in Pervishons and ree stowing the Holes. At Evning we gave the other watch Leff for 48 Hours and I went then. On the 6th Clean All Decks. On the 7th Divine Servis in the fornoon Bind All Small Sails Scrub Hammocks and wash Cloase. In the Evning on the 9th We took the Captains Lady Belonging to *the Phaeton* and famley On Board this Ship and the Captain Belonging to *the Phaeton* took Our Commanders Lady and famley On Board His Ship As It Is Not A Lowed for Any Captain to take His Wife To Sea with Him But they can take a friend. In the afternoon we Let Go of our Morings And A Steamer took Us in Tow and all the Rest of Our Ships was towed Out of Harbour. Verey Light wind all Night. The steamer Let Go of us In the Evning. On the 10th thear was a Steamer Brought Out from Malta 3 Marines that we left at Malta On the 10thA Verey fine day and a Strong Breeze . In the fornoon We Shifted the fortopsail in 4 Minits and we was first ship. In the Evning riff topsails. On the. 11th the Breeze Not So Strong . General Quarters. In the fornoon Wash Cloase at Night. On the 12th A Light Breeze and a fair wind. Set studding sails lower and A Loaft. In the Evning take In all studding sails and reff topsails.

On the 13th A Strong Breeze Holey Stone All Decks In the Morning Watch. In the fornoon We Had A Dubell riff topsail and We Shifted the Main topsails in 6 Minits and 36 secunds. In the Evning Cloast rifft the topsails and we took in one riff in the Courses and we shook out the riffs Again and made sail and then we was In all Most a Ded Calm. On the 14th About 2 Oclok A M we was forst to take in all sails and Point the yards to windurd. Lightning and thunder Verey Hevvy and fast.

Not Much rain. In the Morning watch Make Sail Again . In the fornoon we had the Second Part of It. Again take in all sail and Lower the topsail yards On the Caps A Dubell Riff topsail Breeze all Day. In the Night the Wind Not So Strong. November 15th A Light Breeze. Shift Mizen topsail in 3 Minits and 25 Seconds. On the 16th A fine Morning In the fornoon thear was a Steamer brought out Straigelers from Malta for the fleet. We Had 3 Marines and 2 sailors Cum on Board Our Ship and we Still Leave One Sailor Behind. A Strong Breeze all day. On the 17th A Strong Breeze and a Hevey Swell. Shipt the Main Sail in 5 Minits and 30 seconds. The next ship to us was 6 minits. Blowing a Strong Breeze All Day. On the 18th A fine Morning and we Sited the Island of Majorca. A Strong Breeze . We had general Quarters in the fornoon. Crussing off Portmahon All Night.

On the 19th A fine Morning. Not so much Wind. Crusing off Portmahon. On the 20th A fine Morning. More wind than thear was Last Night. We Caried Away Our Main tagalant sail Before Breakfast and we Caried Away Our Jib in the fornoon. Under Dubell riff topsails all day off Portmahon. In the morning on the 21st Divine Servis. In the fornoon Blowing A Verey Strong Breeze. On the 22nd A Verey Strong Breeze . Cloase riff topsails. In the afternoon we sent Down tagalant yards and Struck the tagalant Masts and furald all sails Except the Main topsail and that was Cloase rifft. We am Now Under Cloase riff Main topsail and For and Main Staisells And then it was Blowing A Gale of Wind. We Hav staid the formast. Lightning at Night But No Rain.

On the 23rd About one Oclok A M We set the for and Mizen topsails. The Wind Not So Strong But A Verey Nastey Swell. Our topsails is Cloase rifft and we are Carreing our Stasells Still. In the fornoon we set Our Courses One riff in them. We took off the Stasells. A Strong Breeze All Day Untill the Evning and then A Light Breeze. We shook out our riffs in the topsails/ A Light Breeze in the first watch but A Nasty Hevey Swell. On the 24th A fine Morning and a Strong Breeze. We hav 3 riffs in our Topsails now. We sent up the tagalant Mast this Morning . In the fornoon about 6 Bells we took in that riff that we shook out yesterday about One Oclok P M . It was Blowing a Strong Gale. We furald the for and Mizen topsails and Staid the for and Main Masts. In the Evning the Wind Bated a Littell and we set the for and Mizen topsails. And the for was Soon Spliet and we soon Bent Another In Its Plase. Its Blowing Verey Strong Now But it is Nearly a fair wind for Gibralter.

On the 25th A fine Morning And A Strong Breeze. After Breakfast we sent up tagalant Mast and yards and made Sail. General Quarters in the fornoon. Dubell riff topsails. Light Breeze all Night. On the 26th A Verey fine Morning. Scrub Hammocks and wash Cloase. A Verey Light Breeze all day. Send Down royal yards in the Evning. On the 27th A fine Morning And A Light Breeze. Holey Stone All Decks In the Morning and fornoon watches. In the Evning In A Ded Calm riffd topsails and Shipt Courses in 4 minit and 30 seconds. In the first watch thear Was A Good Breeze Sprung Up. On the 28th A fine Morning and a Good Breeze rain at times. In the afternoon We Had Lime Dues to day. On the 29th A Squaly Morning A Strong Breeze and Sum rain in the Morning. A fine afternoon and Evning. Dubell riff top-sails at Evning A Strong Breeze All Night. On the 30th A Strong Breeze all Day untill Evning and then a Light Breeze. In the Middell Watch thear was a Steamer Cum from the rock with Our Mail and we laid tow all night.

On the first of December we recived Our Mail and Made Sail Again for the rock of Gibralter. Just off Cape Cadet a Strong Dubell riff topsail Breeze All Night. December 2nd A fine Morning and a Strong Breeze . General Quarters. In the fornoon A Verey Hevvy Swell and a fowell wind for the rock. Dubell riff topsails all day. Verey Cold to What We Hav Bean yousto. In a ded Calme all Night. Wash Cloase at Night On the 3rd in a Ded Calm all day and Night. On the 4th in a Ded Calm all day and Night. On the 5th Morning in a Ded Calm. In this fornoon thear was A Littell Breeze Sprung Up. We set Studing sails Lower and A Loaft. Divine Servis in the fornoon. In a ded Calm all day and Night In the afternoon we was 3 or 4 Miles Behind the Admiral and He Made a Signal for Us and *the Bellerophon* to Prepur for towing and Us shortend and fural sail and By that time thear was a steamer redy to take us in tow and she took us Both and she towed us About 4 or 5 Miles untill we was In Our Station and then the steamer Let Go Of Us and we made Sail. On the 6th A fine Morning In A Ded Calm But About Dinertime We Had A Little Breeze Spring Up and we Made all Sail. Set studding sails Lower and A Loaft. But We Soon Loast All the wind and we furild sails and thear was a Steamer took us and the Britania In tow and A Nother took *the trafalger* and *Albion* In tow . We was Just Off Almaria At the time. In the first (December the 6th 1852)Watch We Past Malaga. The Steamer was towing us 5 and a Hallf Nots per Hour All Night. All Night in a ded Calm All Night. On the 7th at day Breake we sited the rock of Gibralter And Soon After 1 Bell in the Fornoon we Dropt Anchor and Mored Ship. On Bent All Small Sails Got out Our Boom Boats and Comenced staying the Mast and setting up the rigging. We Left Malta on the 9th of Last Month. That makes 28 days We Hav Bean Going from Malta to the Rock of Gibralter About 11 Hundred Miles. We Hav Had Lime Dues served out to us Everscines we left Malta.

On the 8th A Verey fine Morning. *The Bellerophon* Cum in to Harbour About 2 Oclok A M. Setting up the riggin all day. On the 9th we finished setting up the riggin and we set up the Gallant Mast. In the fornoon Getting in Water Boats and Pervishons Untill 12 O clok P M. On the 10th A Cloudey Morning . Holey Stone All

Decks Scrub Hammocks and wash Cloas. After Diner we was Preparing for sea. In the Evning we Got In the Launch and Bent All Small Sails. Rain all the Evning. On the 11th A fine Morning. Watch and Idlers Scrub and Wash Decks. After Breakfast we sent up the Galant and royal Yards and then the Watch Below to Man the Capstan and the watch On Deck to get in the Boom Boats. We got up our anchor and shorten In the Cabel of the Other. At 4 Bells in the fornoon Pipe all Hands Up anchor and after we Had got the anchor well secured We was Cheerd by all the Ships That Has Bean In Company With Us and then we Made Sail and we (had)a Good Breeze and a fair wind through the Gut of Gibralter. *The Phaeton* Friget and A Steamer is going to Lisbon with us. We had studding sails set Lower and Aloaft. We Have Past By trafalger Bay and Cadaz. In the Evning we took in the studding sails [16]. A Strong Breeze all Night.

On the 12th A Dubell Riff topsail Breeze. No Divine Servis. At 2 Bells in the afternoon We was Coat in a Squall. The wind Caried Away Our Crojick yard Before We Could Very Hevey. About 4 Bells the wind Bated A Little and We Made Sail but in the first dog watch we was forst to fural all sails Excepting the Main topsail and He was Cloase Reeft. In the first watch am Under Cloase Reef Main topsail and for and Main staisels . Not much rain . Lightning and rain at times all Night. A Strong Breeze All Night. December the 13th A fine Morning and a strong Breeze. We set a Little sail in the Morning. After Breakfast we sent up the spare Main topsail yard and fited Him as a Crojick yard. The other Crojick yard was Broke Off in two where the slings goes. In the afternoon just befor 4 Bells we furald all sail Except the Main topsail. We set staisells and then Pipe Down Hammocks and by 4 Oclok it did rain verey hevey. At P M the wind Bated a Little but rain verey Hevey But the rain Beate Down the sea a greate deal. At 8 Bells we Weard ship. Very Hevey rain.

On the 14th A fine Morning. After Breakfast Watch wear ship and afterwards Hands make sail. In the Evning reef topsails. On the 15th A Verey fine Morning rather a Strong Breeze. We sited Lisbon in the fornoon. We Crossed Over the Bar about 3 Bells in the afternoon and we dropt anchor in the river tagus. Furald sails. We was then about 5 or 6 miles from the Harbour Of Lisbon. We can see the town Quit Plain. On the 16th Call the watch at 4 Oclok A M. Wash Decks. Pipe Lash up Hammocks after the decks was dun at 3 Bells. After Breakfast at 5 Bells turn the Hands up. Watch Below to the Capstain to Shorten In Cabel and thear was a Steamer Cum A Long side of Us and took Us in tow after our anchor was up and we got On the Way and so did the rodney and Prince reagent. Steamers Had got they in tow. We got out Opasite the Light House on the Bar and thear as the Curant and Swell was so Strong the rodney and Us Careyed away one of our Hausers and we was forst to Make Sail and Put our Ship about the Best way as we

Could and Run Back to our Anchorage Again and Dropt anchor All of Us and fural sails. On the 17th Turn the Hands Up at 5 Oclok. Lash up Hammocks and Pipe to Breakfast. After Breakfast wash Cloase and afterwards wash Down Decks. Now in the river thear is *the Prince reagent* 90 *the rodney* 91 and us 84 guns Each and *the Phaeton* friget 50 guns and 2 steamers. In harbour is *the Sasperall*. On the 18th we turnd the Hands Up at 5 Oclok A M. Pipe Lash Up Hammocks and Pipe to Breakfast and after Breakfast Hands Holey Stone All Decks. We recived 2 days Fresh Pervishons to day and it is much Better Hear than it was at the rock . At 3 Oclok in the Afternoon we got our anchor and *the furey* steamer took Us in tow and she took us out the River tagas and when we was Out Clear She Let Go of Us and we Made Sail and *the Phaeton* Cum out after us and she and us Lay two all Night for the reast of the Ships to join us.

December the 19th A Verey fine Morning and a good Breeze. We sited the Admirals Ship and Others at 2 Bells in the fornoon watch 9 Oclok A M [17] . We went to Divishons at 3 Bells But No Divine Servis For We was forst to Keep the Lower Deck Ports Down. We Took Up Our Station in Rear Of the Admiral in the Wether Line And Made Sail At 7 Bells In the Fornoon. A Strong Breeze All Day And A fair wind For England. Reef topsails at Evning . At 2 Bells In the Last Dog Watch we took in another reef. Under Dubell reef topsails all Night. On the 20th A Fair Morning and a Light Breeze But a Fair Wind. We Aird Bedding at 6 Bells In the fornoon Pipe to Lash Up and Store Hammocks at 2 Bells in the afternoon watch. When we was Up in the Mediterranean Us and *the Phaeton* Frigget Beate All Of the Other Ships Both In Excersise and Sailing.

We did Consider the Frigget and Us Nearly as One [18] For She Did Beate Us In Sailing And We Did Beate Her in Excersise.Both Her and Us Had Got the New Plan In the topsails and Hav Had them In for More than 12 Months Befor Us Left the Admiral Up In the Mediterranean But Last Night as we was reefing topsails this Admiral saw it and He Made A Signal to us and *the Phaeton* for to Put in Our Points in our topsails. He thought of taking us A Back By Doing so But We Had Our topsails Afitted By one Oclok To day. He Made a Signal At 4 Bells in the Afternoon for Us and the Frigget to Shift topsails as He thought we hadnt got them fitted But we was waiting for sumthing. We was 5 Minits a Shifting our Mizen and 5 minits and 30 seconds at the for and 6 minits at the Main topsail Complate in 6 minits. *The Phaeton* was 10 Minits Complating. Not Verey Much wind at the time But a Verey Hevey Swell. Reef topsails in the Evning. We was the first Ship *the Phaeton* next. On the 21st A fine Morning and a fair wind But A Light Breeze. In the fornoon the Admiral Made A Signal for All the Captains to go On Board His Ship To Pass sum Midshipmen for Meats. Rain in the Evning. Reef topsails after Super and we was the first ship. It is Verey Cold Now to us As we am just cum from a Hot Climent.

December 22nd A fine Morning and A Strong Breeze. At 6 Bells in the fornoon we was going 12 Knots Per Hour. At 7 Bells we floged a Sailor. He recived 48 lashes and to be sent A Shoar with a Blanck Discharge when we do arive in England. In the afternoon at 3 Bells We Doubell reeft topsails and then it was Blowing a Verey Strong Breeze. On the 23rd Morning about 2 Oclok the Officer of the watch got the Ship Out Of Her Station and When we got Her In Her Station We was Many A Mile A Sturn Of the Other Ships. After Breakfast we Made Sail and Got to Our Distance from the Other Ships At 4 Bells In the fornoon. We took in 2 reefs in our topsails as All the Reast Had got them In And Just as we Had Dun reefing and the Watch Below Had Got On the Lower Deck the admiral made a Signal for all the fleet to Shift tagalant Masts And Then He Hove Out A Nother to Shift Jib boom and then to Shift Mizen topsail and then to Shift All topsails and Courses. When we Comenst We Had our royal yards A Croast and then we Complated the First Ship in the fleet after all of the triing to Humbugg Us.December the 23rd All the rest of the Other ships had got the Start of us as Non Of them Had thear royal Yards Croast. From the time the Signal was Broake Untill We Had Complated Shifting Evry Thing and got all the sails set we was One Hour and 2 minits and 10 seconds. The rodney was 1 Hour 13 Minits and 30 seconds. *The Prince reageant* was 1 Hour 19 Minits and 20 Seconds. All the Reast Was Much Longer. Befor sum of them had finished it was Blowing A Strong Breeze A Dobell Reef topsail Breeze Befor and after rain in the afternoon.

In the Evning wash Cloase them that Lick. On the 24th A Strong Breeze and a fair wind Up the English Channel. General Quarters in the fornoon. After quarters we tried for soundings and we found soundings in 42 fathom of water. A fine wind all day. When we was at General Quarters we could not Woork the Lower Deck Guns for we was Ablidge to keep the Lower Deck ports Down as the Ship was roling so Hevey. Ships in Company from Lisbon to England is *the Prince reagent* flying Admiral Currys flag and *the rodney* and us 2 Deckers *the Phaeton* friggett and *the termagent* steam Frigget and *the furey* steamer. *The Phaeton* Had One Man Kild while at Excersise on the 23rd.

December 25th 1852 A Verey Strong Breeze in the Morning Watch. Running Under Cloase reef topsails All Night. After Day brake we made sail and By Breakfast time we Sited the Isal of Waight and we got to Spit Hed about 4 Oclok in the afternoon and Dropt anchor and furald sails and Pipe to super [19]. After super we (Had) A Exter Lowines of grogg Servd Out to us. Lights and Smoaking untill 9 Oclok P M And the Band A Plaing Untill 9 Oclok. Rain in the Evning. On the 26th A Fine Morning. Thear was One of Our Marines Died about 5 Bells in the Morning Watch. He was Sick for 3 or 4 Months. Sent up tagalant yards at 8 Oclok. Divitions and Divine Servis in the fornoon.

Home Waters and a Refit

Womans A Lowed On Board. They Left the Ship in the Evning. It Cum on to Blow Verey Hevey just Befor 12 Oclok in the first watch. We Keept Anchor Watch All Night. We Dropt Our Best Bower Anchor about 12 Oclok. On the 27th About 2 Bells in the Morning Watch We Let Go Our Stabuard Shut Anchor. A Pipe to Strick Lower yards and topmast and then it was Blowing All Most A Hurican and Rain A Littel After we Had Sent Down the Mast and yards. Pipe to Breakfast. In the afternoon the Wind Bated A Littell and we got up the Shut anchor. Keep No Anchor Watch that Night. On the 28th A Verey fine Morning. At 8 Oclok we Sent Up the Lower yards and Topmasts and tagalant Masts and Yards and Loost sails and at 2 Bells in the afternoon we furald them. Send down tagalant yards in the Evning. The termagant steamer went in to Harbour to day. On the 29th A fine Morning. Holey Stone Uper and Main Decks and Clean Lower Deck. In the fornoon we got out the Pennaces and took that Marine that died A few Days ago to Haslar and Buried Him and just after they Left the Ship it Cum on to Blow Verey Hevey and rain. We struck the galant Mast. The Boat Scrous Could not Cum Off To the Ship Untill the Next Day the 30th. Rain in the morning of the 30th Turn the Hands Up at 3 Bells in the Morning Watch. Scrub and Wash Decks. We sent up the tagalant Masts tagalant and royal Yards and Loost Sails at 2 Bells in the fornoon. Fural Sails at 6 Bells. The Ship Rights Cum On Board to Examine Our Decks . Send Down the gallant and royal yard at sunset. Scrub and wash Cloase. A fine Evning. December 31st Scrub and Wash Decks after Breakfast. Rain in the fornoon No General Quarters but Exercisin with Small Arms In the Afternoon Leff for All Married Men and for the First Section of Boath Watches for 24 Hours. Rain in the Evning.

(January 1st 1853 [20]) Turn the Hands Up at 5 Oclok A M. Lash Up Hammocks and Pipe to Breakfast. After Breakfast Wett Holey stone the Uper and Main Decks and Dry Holey Stone the Lower Deck. In the fornoon thear was 2 Masters Cum from the Dock yard and Examind our ropes and sails and Baggs as they was going to be Condemid. In the Afternoon our Commander Left Us. His Permoshing (promotion) Is Cum On Board to Him As Post Captain. We Cheerd Him as He Left the Ship. His name is M R Mends [21]. In the Evning Verey Cold and we Do fell it as we am just from a Hot Station. On the 2nd a Weet Morning. Divine Servis in the fornoon. Leff in the afternoon for so Many to go On Shoar as is Cum Off that went on Leff On Friday and Saturday But that was not Many. On the 3rd A Weet Morning But It Cleard away in the fornoon and we Loosd sails and the Water taink Cum A Long

Side with 55 tons of Water for us. Fural sails at 7 Bells in the afternoon. Fine ever sines the Morning .January the 4th A Strong Wind. Strick the Galant Masts at 2 Bells in the Morning Watch. This Moorning we sent One of our Pinnaces Ashoar to Portsmouth For the Liberty Men But they Could Not Cum Off Befor they was towed Out to Spit Head By A Steamer.In the afternoon we got In the Pinnace.

On the 5th A fine Morning. Sent up the gallant Masts and tagalants and royal yards and Loost sails. *The furey* steamer Went In To Harbour this afternoon. Fural sails at 7 Bells in the fornoon. Very Cold In The Evning. On the 6th Turn the Hands Up at 3 Bells And Pipe to Breakfast at 4 Bells. After Breakfast the Watch On Deck A scrubing Uper and Main decks The watch Below Dry Holey stoning the Lower Deck. Rain and Blow Verey Hevey. At 7 Bells in the fornoon we sent down the tagalant Masts. In the Evning Not So Much wind nor rain. Scrub Hammocks and Wash Cloase from 7 Oclok untill 9 at night. On the 7th a weet morning. Rain and Blow Verey Hevey all day. Make and Mend Cloase or smoking which we Liek all day. In the Evning it Cleard Off fine and we Hung Up Our Hammocks and Cloase to Dry them.

On the 8th A Fine Morning and all day. We got the Hammocks Dry to day. In the Evning Leff for A watch to go On Shoar for 48 Hours. In the afternoon thear was A Liter Cum from Navel yard and took sum Condemed Breid from Our Ship. January 9th A fine morning. Watch on the Uper Deck Scrub and Wash the Uper and Main Decks. Watch below clean the Lower Deck. Divine Servis in the fornoon . Fine all day. On the 10th A weet Morning. Clean all Decks. Rain and Blow Verey Hevvy all day. Very few Liberty Men Cum Off to Day. On the 11th rain and Blow All Day. We Had Orders this Morning to Preaper for sea and we Bent Small sails and got in our Boom Boats and got in our Commadation Lader and riged the Davids at 7 Bells in the Afternoon we struck our Lower yards and topmasts and it was Blowing Verey Strong. We Had Another Commander Cum On Board to day and take Charge. On the 12th A Strong Wind all day and rain at times. Our Mast and Yards Have Been down all day. On the 13th A fine Morning But A Strong Breeze. Clean all Decks. At 8 Oclok send up Lower yards and topmasts and tagalant Masts and yards and set up topmast riggin and Loos sails. *The Phaeton* friget Got Up Her anchor at 12 Oclok And Saild Past By Our Sturn and We Cheerd Her and She Cheerd Us As She Past By Us. We bent Studding Sail gear in the fornoon. We have Had A Longer Spull Hear than we Hav Sines We Left the rock of Gibralter In April Last.

Ships now at Spit Hed Is 3 Line of Battell Ships and 5 friggets English and A Russian frigget. In the afternoon we got in a Another Croggick yard in the Plase of that one that we Caried away while Cumming from the rock to Lisbon. On the 14th A fine Morning. General Quarters. In the fornoon the Captain Cum On Board at 12

Oclok and as soon as He was On Board the Hands was turnd up Watch Below Man the Captsain watch on deck to the Cat and fish foll After we had up 1 anchor and shortend in the Cabell of the other the Pipe went watch Below up anchor, Watch on deck Make sail[22]. We saild towards the Nab Light and after we got to the Back of the Isal of Waight we Had a good Breeze and a fair wind for Plymouth. A Strong Breeze All Night. On the 15th A Dubell reef topsail Breeze. In the Evning Cloase reef for and Main topsails and stasells and fural Mizen topsail. A Strong Breeze All Night. On the 16th A Weet Morning. The wind Not So Strong. No Divine Servis as it did Rain So Hevey. Fine in the Afternoon. A Light Wind and a Beating wind for us to Plymouth. In the Last dog watch in all Most a ded Calm but Befor Morning we Had More wind. January 17th A fine Morning But A Cold Wind. Almost A fair Wind. We Sited Edaston Light House by Dinertime. Shook Out 3 reefs in Our topsail in the fornoon. In the afternoon take in one of them and we took In the Harbour Master this afternoon Out Side of the Breake Water. We Got inside of the Breakewater by 3 Bells in the first Dog Watch and Shorten sail and Dropt Our Best Bower Anchor and furald Sails and squard yards and Sent Down the tagalant yards and Cleared Up the Decks and Pipe to Super And Down All Hammocks.

On the 18th A fine Morning. Turn the Hands Up at 3 Bells and Pipe to Breakfast at 4 Bells and after Clean Decks. At 9 Oclok A M we salluted the Port admiral and then Loost Sails. In the afternoon we Onbent all the small sails Un furald the topsails and Courses and the Powder Ligter Cum Along Side Of Us and took Out Our Powderand Shell. We Had More than 30 tons of Powder in our Magazine. On the 19th A weet Morning. After Breakfast Scrub and Wash all Decks. After Quarters getting all the Cutlashes and Pistols and Small Arms redey for returning to the Dock yards.

January the 19thWatch Below shorten In Cabell. At 7 Bells thear was 2 steamers Cum along side Of Us and we Got Up the anchor and the Harbour Master with the 2 steamers took Us In to Harbour and Lashed Us A Longside of *the Vigo* Hulk. Pipe to Diner at 6 Bells In the Afternoon. About 5 Oclok we Piped To Stand By Hammocks and as the Captain gave Leff to Petty Officers and Good Conduct Men and not to the watch as yousaral Thear Was Agreat Many Men that would not go off the Lower Decks for thair Hammocks and the men on the Lower Deck Put Out all the Lights and Broake a Great Deale of thair Mess Things in the for Part of the Lower Deck. The royal Marines aft was Verey Quiet. Thay Pipd to Stand By Hammocks and non of them would Obay the Pipe but Keep Shouting. The Commander and first Lieutenant and Captain Of royal Marines and the Officer Of the guard went all Round all the Decks and they Had Lights with them But Sum of them was soon Put Out And Lanterns Smashed. Thay Planted Sentenals All Round the Lower and Main

Decks and Beate To Divishons. All the royal Marines a fell In on the Lower Deck. The Comander Put 2 or 3 of the ringladers In Irons And then Pipe to Stand By Hammocks and Clear the A Party at the Dockyard At Woork. On the 26th a weet Morning but fine about Mid Day. A Party at the Dock Yard Drawing Stors And Bringing them off to Main and Lower Decks then they went After thair Hammocks[23].

On the 20th A fine Morning. Turn the Hands up at 3 Bells. Pipe to Breakfast at 4 Bells After Breakfast Holey Stone Uper and Main Decks . Clean Lower Deck at 9 Oclok. On Bent all gun gear and Loos the topsails and Courses. At 3 Bells in the afternoon the Captain of the flag Ship Cum on Board of Our Ship and Mustered the Ships Company and we got up all the sails that was In the sail room and returned them to the Hulks. At 7 Bells we on bent the topsails and Courses and returned them to the Hulk. In the Evning Leff for A watch to go on shoar untill next Morning 7 Oclok. On the 21st A Damp Morning. Clean Decks as Befor At 8 Oclok A M Pipe Down Lower yards and Topmast and return the gear to the Hulk such as the Boatswans Stors and gear that we Hav Had in youse Latly. In the afternoon so Weet that the Hands could not woork on Deck thear was Betwen 60 and 70 men that went on Leff Last Night that Did Not Cum off to thair Leff this Morning. A fine Evning. Leff to the Other watch.to go On Shoar untill the next Morning at 7 Oclok A M Last Evning thear was a Sailor Brought On Board that run from us at Malta and Now He Is In Irons In the for Cokpit. He got to Woork By Day and Sleep in Irons By Night. Returning guners and Carpenters and Boatswains stors as Long as we could See and then Pipe to super. After super Pipe Down Hammocks.

On the 22ndA fine Morning. In the fornoon taking the Officers Cheasts Out and Clearing Out the Cabins and Taking It Over to the Hulks. After Diner Pipe all Mess things over to the Hulk. In the Evning gave Leff for the watch to Go On Shoar untill Monday Morning at 7 Oclok. Thear is a Great Many Men Ashoar A Breaking thair Leff that went the first Leff this Night. All that was on Board slept On Board the Hulk for the first time. On the 23rd A fine Morning. Turn the hands Up at 4 Bells and Lash up Hammocks and Stow them Down in the Holloop Deck. At 3 Bells in the fornoon watch Beate for Divishons and after Divishons Leff for aney One that Did Not Breake their Leff At Ship Hed. More than 70 Hours Leff Untill To Morrow Morning 7 Oclok Verey fine all day. January the 24th A Verey fine Morning and thear was about 20 Corkers Cum on Board and Comensd Corking Our Decks. And we sent a Party to the Dock to Return Stors and Draw New in the Plase of Old. On the 25 A fine Morning. The Corkers is A Corking the Outside of the Ship. the Ship. On the 27thA fine Morning. Watch below Clearing the liter and Watch On Deck reefitting the reggin and reefitting all running gear. Leff Evry Evning for A watch Untill next Morning at 7 Oclok.

On the 28th A fine Morning. Examin the Cabells and send them Below again. Thar is a Party of Men A Scraping after the Corkers. In the afternoon the Captain of the flag Ship Cum on Board and Mustered Our Ships Company. Thear was a few men absent but not Many. We Onshipt our after Captsains And Sent It Ashoar as the Spindal of It was Splut. It was sent Ashoar to be Repaird . On the 29th A Fine Morning. The scraping party at thair woork and a Party A getting Up Cabell and after it is Examind send it Down again. In the afternoon Clean all Decks. In the Evning Leff for aney one that havnot Broke thair Leff in Plymouth untill Monday Morning.

On the 30th A fine Morning. Pipe to Breakfast as Yousurl. Clean the Uper Deck of the Hulk. Divine Servis in the fornoon. Leff for aney One that Havnot Broke thair Leff Hear from this afternoon untill tomorrow Morning at 7 Oclok. Rain in the Afternoon. Thear was a Greate Many Visaters Cum On Board to day to see the Ships Company. On the 31st A fine Morning. The Scraping Party at woork in the ship. In the afternoon the Uper and Main Deck Quarters A Scraping thair Guns. In the Evning scrub and wash the Uper and Main Decks. The Corkers Havnot Quit finishd the Lower Deck. In the Evning Leff for watch. To day thear was sumthing fell from A Loaft And Struck A Man But Not To Hurt Much.

On the first of February 1853 A fine Morning. The scraping party A scraping the Main Deck where it was white washed and about 20 Marines Out side of the ship a Puddying the seams. The Boatswain at the Dock yard Drawing stors for the Ship. Painting the Quarter Deck guns and shot in the afternoon. In the Evning wash the Main Deck. He Corkers finished On Board to day but thear is sum Carpenters at woork still from the Dock yard.February the 2nd A damp morning. The scraeping and puddeing party at woork. Painting the Main deck to day. On the 3rd A wet Morning. Painting the Main Deck. Rain all day. Muster the Ships Company at 1 Oclock P M. On the 4th A fine Morning. Scrub one watches Hammocks and Hang them Up. After Breakfast Painting one side of the Ship Out side and Painting the Lower Deck gun Carriages. Leff for the watch as befor. On the 5th A fine Morning. After Breakfast Painting the Out side of the Ship and we dun painting all the guns to day. The other watches Hammocks scrubd in the fornoon. Leff for the watch untill Monday Morning at 7 Oclok. On the 6th Verey fine Morning. Divisions at 3 Bells in the fornoon. No Divine Servis. A Verey fine Day thear was a great Many Visiters off to this Ship to day. On the 7th A weet Morning. Painting the Main Deck and A Party A Stowing away Sails in the Sail room. On the 8th A weet Morning.

Home Leave
The Pay yatch Dropt Along side of the Hulk at 8 Oclok A M. And they Commensd Paying the Ships Company about 10 Oclok AM. I was Paid about 1 Oclok and I Left

the Hulk about 4 Oclok PM and I took the train at 6 PM for Bristol and I got thear about 12 Oclok Mid Night and I stopt thear all Night[24]. On the 9th Morning At Bristol I took the train and went throu Bath to Chiptman and thear I took another train to froom and I stopd thear that Night. On the Evning of the 10th I got Home All Safe and I was Verey glad to find all My frends so well as I did. On the 11th father and Me went to Shepton Mallett Market. On the 16th Benjamin and Me went to froom Market. All Other times I Injoid My Sellf Verey Much Sum times Out A Shutting And Other Injoiments All the time While I was on Leff.

On the 22nd Left Home about 8 Oclok AM and Benjamin and Me for Stratton and I left Stratton about A Hallf Past 9 Oclok the same Morning and I arived at Bath 5 Minets Past 11 Oclok. And I took the Express train at Hallf Past 12 Oclok for Plymouth and I arived at Plymouth about Hallf Past 5 Oclok PM. And I stopped Ashoar untill the 26th of the Same Month and then in the Evning Me and 3 or 4 More Marines Went On Board all right and We that went On Board that Night was forgave for Being Absent and all that Cum off After that Night was Punnished for all the time they was ashoar Abreaking thair Leff. On the 26th No Divine Servis. Verey Cold. On the 27th Holey stone all decks and Divishons at 9 Oclok A.m and at One Bell in the afternoon watch thear was A greate Maney of Our Men Not Cum off yet But they am Absent Ever Sines the 22nd of this Month . Today the Captain of the flag Ship Musterd Our Ships Company And He found a greate Maney of Our Men absent.

Back on Duty
On the first of March 1853 A Dull Morning and all day. On the 2nd A fine Morning and Holey stone all Decks and Painting Ship. On the 3rd We Hoisted our Main Lower yard to get in sum Pervishons and we Complated 4 Months Pervishons. Our Captain is on Leff Still. On the 4th Morning About 1 Oclok AM thear was A fire Ashoar And We Turnd the Hands Up and Cald the Boats Crus Away and we got 2 of Our fire Engines in the Boats but the Boats did not Land them. The fire was Put Out Befor they Could Arive thear. After Breakfast Divishons and then Quarters and after Holey stone the Hulks Lower Deck. In the Afternoon Holey Stone the Hulks Main Deck and yards. Getting in Coals in our Ship. Rain in the Evning.Leff for any Of Us that Havnot Broke thair Leff. I could go Ashoar if I Lick. I hear that there was 2 lives Lost at the Fire this morning.

March the 5th Turn the Hands up at 4 Bells and Pipe to Breakfast at 5 Bells. Beat to Divishons at 1 Bell in the fornoon and Holey stone the Lower Deck, In the aftwernoon Holey stone the Main and Upper Deck and getting in Carpenters stors. Leff for Both Watches to go On Shoar Untill Monday Morning. On the 6th A Dull Morning. Divishons at 5 Bells In the fornoon. No Divine Servis. Rain In the Evning. On the 7th A fine Morning. Turn the Hands up at 4 Bells Pipe to Breakfast at Quarter to 5 Bells. Hands Clean Main Deck in the Hulk at 6 Bells. Divishons at 1 Bell in the fornoon afterwards Quarters and Cleaning Wood work and Dry up all Deck. Our Captain Cum on Board this Morning And He Musterd the Ships Company and He found a Greate Many Absent. On the 8th A weet Morning. Quarters at 1 Bell Quarters at 2 PM. Afterwards Dry up Decks and ree stowing Booms. We Hav 4 Stoves On Our Lower Deck by day with fire in them to Dry the deck. Leff as befor. On the 9th A fine Morning. Turn the Hands up at 4 Bells. Breakfast Divishons Quarters As Befor. In the fornoon Shipt All Sails from the Hulk to the Ship. In the afternoon getting in Coals. Thear was a greate Maney Men Cum round from Portsmouth In A Steamer to day. Sum Of them Hav Been Absent Ever sines the 22nd of Last Month. That Man and his Daughter was Buried yesterday that was Burnt to Deth in the Last fire ashoar. On the 10th A fine Morning. Turn the Hands up and Pipe to Breakfast Quarters and Divishons as yousuall. In the fornoon Holey stone the Hulks Main and Hollop Decks. In the afternoon Holey stone the Ships Uper and Main Decks. Leff in the Evning as YouserelL.

On the 11th A fine Morming. Turn the Hands up and Pipe to Breakfast and Quarters and Divishons as Yousall. Holeystone Lower Deck of the Ship. In the fornoon the Captain of the flag Ship Musterd Our Ships Company. At 3 Bells in the afternoon Holey stone the Hulks Hollop Deck and getting In Pervishons for the ward and gun room Officers. Getting in Coals In the Evning . We Do Hav Divishons twise a Day Now On A Count of so Many Men going A shoar. On the New Act as us call it – that is going Ashoar with out Leff [25]. There is now in Irons 2 Marines 1 Sailorand 8 or 10 that Do Sleep In the Cells By Night and woork By Day. Thear is a greate Maney of our Marines that Has got Knapsack Drill by Day and Sleep In Chokey By Night. On the 12th A fine Morning. Morning Duty as yousal. In the fornoon Holey stone the Hulks Main and Lower Decks. In the Afternoon Scrub the gun room and scrubing Canvas. In the Evning Leff for Both Watches to go on Shoar untill Monday Morning the 14th Inst. This Evning we slung Clean Hammocks. Thear was one Private and one Drumer of Royal Marines joind us to day. They Cum from Plymouth Barracks. Thay Cum In the Plase of Men that Hav Bean gone to the Hospital more than one month. We shall Want More Next Week In Plase of Men that have run from the ship. On the 13th A fine Morning. Turn the Hands up at 5 Bells. Pipe to Breakfast at 6 Bells. Divishons at 3 Bells In the fornoon. After Divishons Smoaking alowed all Day untill 8 Oclok PM. Rain in the Evning. On the 14th A Verey fine Morning. Turn the Hands up at 4 Bells pipe to Breakfast at 5 Bells. Call the Hands at Quarter past 6 Bells In the fornoon. We sent up forLower yards and topmast and set up topmast riggen. In the afternoon Scrub Boats Gear. Leff for the watch

March 15th A fine Morning. Duty as Befor. In the fornoon We got in the Boom Boats and Squard yards and then Calld the watch for the first time sines I Hav Bean off Leff. And then the watch Sent up the tagalant Masts and squard yards. After diner the Boat Crows Acleaning the Boom Boats and getting the Sails reddy for bending getting sum of the Officers things from the Hulk to the Ship. Leff in the Evning.

On the 16th A fine Morning. Morning Duty as Befor. In the fornoon Bend all Plain Sail and Squard yards and then furald Sails and Squard yards. In the afternoon Shift over all Mess things and Officers things. In the Evning we took over our Hammocks and Baggs. Scrub Hammocks them that Licks. On the 17th A fine Morning. Duty as Befor. After Breakfast Watch On Deck Clean the Uper and Main Decks Watch Below clean the Lower Deck. In the Fornoon cleaning all Decks and Officers Cabins of the Hulk. Verey Cold to day. The Captain of the flag Ship Musterd Our Ships Company at 2 Oclok PM. No Leff this Evning But for Petty Officers and Men that Havnot Broke thair Leff at all and that's not Maney. Pipe down Hammocks at 6 Oclok PM afterwards Hoist Up the Boats The Band Plaing on the Aft Deck Just Out side of the ward room Doar after Diner. In the ward room thay Play Evrey Night After Diner for About a Hour and Hallf Sunday Nights and all other Nightswhen the Captain is Not On Board But when He Is He will Not Alow Of It [26].

On the 18th A Verey Cold Morning. Morning Duty as Befor. At 7 Bells thear was two steamers Cum A Long side of us and took us in tow. At 8 Bells Oclok AM we Cast Off from the Hulk and the Harbour Masters took us Out in the Sound with the steamers and we Dropt Both Anchors at 3 Bells in the fornoon and then Mored Ship. And thear was a shill Lighter Cum A Long side of Our Ship and we Pipt to Diner Just after 6 Bells. At 1 Bell in the afternoon we turnd the Hands Up and Got In our Shill and Powder and it was Late in the Evning when we had Cleard Both Lighters Of Powder and Shill. No Leff. On the 19th A Fine Morning but Verey Cold. Turn the Hands up at 4 Bells. After Breakfast watch on Deck Holey stone uper and Main Decks. Watch Below Holey Stone Lower Deck and Hollop (Orlop) Deck. We sent up the tagalant Masts at 2 Bells in the fornoon watch. At 12 Oclok Mid Day thear was a signal made from the flag Ship for We to Preapear for sea and We Hoisted the Blu Pennant. In the afternon we Bent all Small Sails and we was getting in things for the Officers and thear was 4 More Marines joind us in Plase of sum that rund from us. We sent One Marine ashoar this Evning To Stop Ashoar untill Sessions for thair was a female robd Him When He was Paid Up Last Month and She was sent to Prison untill Sessions and He Has to apear against Her In April following. No Leff for anney one.

On the 20th A fine Morning. Turn the Hands up at 3 Bells. Pipe to Breakfast at 4 Bells. Call all Hands at 6 Bells. Watch on Deck Scrub Uper and Main Decks watch Below Clean Lower Deck. Quarters at 1 Bell in the fornoon. Sent up tagalant yards at 2 Bells and squard yards. Divishons at 4 Bells. No Divine Servis as we Hav No Chaplin nor Captain On Board. Getting in Sheep and Fowells for the Captain and Other Officers. Send down the tagalant yards at sunset. On the 21st A fine Morning. Duteys as yesterday. After Breakfast watch on Deck Clearing Pervishon Lighter. Quarters at 1 Bell Divishons at 2 Bells and then it was raining and Snowing. At 7 Bells Fine. Turn the Hands Up and sent up the tagalant yards and Loosd Sails. In the afternoon Clean arms and A clearing boats of Pervishons and Fowell for the Officers. At 7 Bells in the afternoon fural sails and send Down tagalant yards and Hoist Up all Boats. In the Evning after Super Scrub Hammocks and wash Cloase. On the 22nd Verey Cold. Turn the Hands up at 2 Bells . Haing up Hammocks and Pipe to Breakfast. Scrub and wash Decks as yesterday. Sent up the tagalant yards at 2 Bells. The Captan Cum On Board this fornoon. Return our clean Hammocks . This Evning send down tagalant yards. Last Evning the Purcer Paid 2 months Shoart alowanes money to the Ships Company. This Evning thear was 3 More Marines joind this Ship. That maks 16 sines we Hav Bean Hear. On the 23rd A fine Morning. Turn the Hands up at 3 Bells. Morning Duty as yesterday of cleaning Decks. Quarters and Divishons. Send up tagalant yards at 2 Bells. Inspect all Small Arms to day. To Day the (?) was Launched. She is to Carey 100 or 101 guns On 2 Decks.

March the 24th A very fine Morning. Turn the Hands up at 3 Bells. Pipe to Breakfast. Wash Decks and Quarters as yesterday. Send up tagalant & royal yards. At 2 Bells this fornoon the Captain of *the queen* Cum On Board this Ship and Musterd us all at our Stations for Loosing and Making Sail. Afterwards our Commander asked Permishon to Excersise New raised Men and It was A Granted. We Loosed and Made Sail Shortn and fural sail, watch square yards. After Diner Clearing Boats and Pipe Make and Mend Cloase. At sunset send down tagalant and royal yards and tagalant masts. No Leff. On the 25th A Verey Cold and weet Morning. Snow and rain all the Morning. Morning Duty as yousarell. Clean arms at 1 Bell in the fornoon. Beate to Divitions at 3 Bells. No Divine Servis for we hav No Chaplan On Board. Smoking All Day Keept as Sunday. It was good Friday. No Leff. On the 26th A fine Morning but Verey Cold. Morning Duty as Befor. At 8 Oclok Hoist and Breake the Ensign and send up the gallant masts and yards. Watch set up the tagalant riggen and Squar yards. Clean arms at 1 Bell. Quarters at 2 Bells. Clear Lower deck. Afternoon A Loose and Make sail and then fural sail and Lower and topmast Studding sails All Night. On the squar In the afternoon watch on Deck Holey stone Uper and Main Decks. Our Captain Has Been On Board to day. Sling Clean Hammocks this Evning. No Leff for any One.

On the 27th A Verey fine Morning. Morning Duty as yesterday. Sent up the tagallant yards at 8 Oclok Quarters at 1 Bell Divitions at 4 Bells . The Captain was at Divitions. Divine Servis in the fornoon. Leff for any one that hasnot Broke thair Leff sines the long Leff untill to morrow Morning 8 Oclok. We Hav Had a frish Chaplin join us sins we hav bean In the Sound. Beate to Quarters at 3 Bells in the first Dog watch. Afterwards Send Down tagalant yards and Hoist up All Boats. On the 28th A fine Morning but rather cold. Morning Duty as Befor. Send Up tagalant yards at 8 Oclok and bent galant gear and squar yards. In the fornoon thear was 2 steam friggets Cum in to the Sound from Spit Hed. Thear names is *Sidon and Lepord. The Prince Reagent* Hove in Side of the Breake Water About 2 Bells in the Afternoon. Scrub Hammocks and wash Cloase in the Evning. No Leff for Officers Nor Men. On the 29th A fine Morning. Morning Duty as yesterday. Sent up tagalant yards at 8 Oclok. Clean arms at 1 Bell. All Small Arm Men to Muster with thair Arms in the fornoon and Drill Getting in Mor Pervishons. After diner Stand By Scrubd Hammocks And field Piss Men at Excersise. In the Evning Muster with Our Clean Hammocks and return them and Hoist Up all Boats and Send Down tagalant yards. No Leff. One More Marine joind this Ship to Day.

On the 30th A Verey Cold Morning. Morning Duty as Befor. Sent up tagalant yards at 8 Oclok. Clean Arms . At 1 Bell two rools for Quarters. Afterwards Loos sails. In the Fornoon the Captain Hav Bean On Board for a Few Hours. He Cums Most Days for a short time and then go Ashor Again. Send Down tagalant yards at Sunset And Hoist up all Boats. Leff for Petty Officers and Non Comishon Officers From 10 Oclok PM Untill 9 Oclok Next Morning. On the 31st A fine Morning. Turn the Hands Up at 2 Bells. Morning Duty as yousarl. At 8 Oclok send up tagalant yards and Loos sails. Clean arms and Divitions as other Days. At 4 Bells Pipe to Make and Mend Cloas. Fural sails at 4 Bells in the afternoon. At 6 Bells send Down tagalant yards and Masts and then It Did Blow and rain Verey Hevey. After Super Quarters. After Quarters Range Shute Cabel and Point the yards to windward and getting all things reddy for stricking lower yards and topmast. Blowing Veret Hevey all Night and we Keept Anchor Watch all Night and we Vard out Cabell 3 or 4 times During the Night.

On the first of April 1853 A Fine Morning the wind Not So Strong. Morning Duty as Befor. Clean arms at 1 Bell General Quarters at 2 Bells Loos sails at 6 Bells Pipe to Diner at 8 Bells. In the Evning Up all Boats. On the 2nd of April A fine Morning. Morning Duty as Befor. Send up tagalant Masts at 8 Oclok and Squard yards. Clean arms at 3 Bells Diner at 12 Oclok Clean Guns at 3 Bells in the afternoon. Thear was a Sailor sent to Exeter Jaiol for 28 days for Stricking the Master at Arms and Ships Corpoarl On Shoar While He was Breaking His Leff. Thear was 2 more Royal Marines joind this Ship to day. Pipe to Super at 3 Bells In the first Dog Watch. After Super to Divishons for the Clean Hammocks and Hoist Up all Boats and Sling Clean Hammocks. Leff for Petty Officers to Go On Shoar in the fornoon and Cum Of to the Ship In the Evning. On the 3rd A Weet Morning. Duty as Befor. Clean arms at 1 Bell in the fornoon Divishons at 3 Bells for Inspection. Divine Servis in the fornoon. Leff For Any One that Havnot Broke thair Leff sines the Long Leff. After Super Send Down tagalant Masts and Inn swinging Booms and Up all Boats. Watch Below range Shute Cable. Pipe down Hammocks afterwards.

On the 4th A fine Morning. Turn the Hands up at 2 Bells Pipe to Breakfast at 3 Bells. Call All Hands a Quarter befor 5 Bells. Watch On Deck Clean Uper and Main Decks watch below Clean Lower Deck. At 8 Oclok 8 Bells send up tagalant Masts. Clean arms at 1 Bell. Afterwards send up tagalant and royal yards at 2 Bells and Loos & Make Sail and Brace round the yards. Squar the yards and Shorten and fural sails. At Sunset sent Down the royal and tagalant yards and Tagalant Masts And then It Did Blow and rain Verey Hevey. Scrub Hammocks and wash Cloase. On the 5th A weet Morning.Turn the Hands up at 1 Bell Pipe to Breakfast at 2 Bells But Non Of the Cooks Of the Messes Would go for thair Cocoa as It was so Long for us to go From Breakfast to Diner time from 5 Oclok in the Morning Untill 12 Oclok Mid Day thay Cald the watch at 4 Bells . Watch Below Clean the Main and Lower Decks. The Cook kept the Cocoa untill 5 Bells and then Non of the Ships Company Did go for the Cocoa and then the Cook recived Orders to Start the Cocoa Over Board and so He Did Clean arms[27] at 1 Bell after 6 Oclok Quarters at 2 Bells. Sent up the tagalant Masts at 4 Bells and Haing up the Clean Hammocks. A Nother Royal Marine joind this Ship this Morning . On the 6th A verey Damp Morning. Turn the watch up at 1 Bell after 4 Oclok the same time as thay turnd All Hands Up yesterday Morning. Now we Hav got the Old ruteen as we Had Got when Our Old Commander Had Got Comand Of Us - that is to turn the watch and Iddelers Up at 4 Oclok Or at 1 Bell after and to wash Or Holey stone Uper and Main Decks. After the Decks as Dried Up and all the Ropes flimished Down Pipe watch and Iddlers Lash up Hammocks. At 4 Bells Pipe up All Hammocks. At 5 Bells Pipe to Breakfast. Quarter to 7 Bells Pipe watch on Deck fall In On the Uper Deck to Muster and watch Below Clean Lower Deck or Holey stone Him as is required. Clean arms at 1 Bell. Quarters Afterwards Drill for the Watch On Deck of the Lower Deck. Quarters on the Main Deck. Loos sails, Drill the Royal Marines and Blu Jackets at Miney Riffel Drill and A firing at targats with field Peses. Fural sails. In the Evning After Super Quarters and Up all Boats. Verey Foggey all Day.

On the 7th A Dull Morning. Morning Duty as yesterday. Loos sails at 8 Oclok AM. Watch below clean Lower Deck. Haing up Hammocks Just Befor 1 Bell. Clean arms at 2 Bells. Divishons at 3 Bells. At 4 Bells the Captain of the Queen Cum On Board Our Ship and Musterd Our Ships Company. Fural Sails and Stand By. Scrub Hammocks. In the Afternoon Leef for any One to go On Shore that Hav Not Broke thear Leef at Plymouth. Admiral Curry went On Board *the Princeregent* and Hoisted his Flag at the Mizen And We Shifted Our Cullers from White to Blu. We am under His Command now. Thear was a Boy floged to Day. He Had 12 Lashes Across His Backside. On the 8th A fine Morning. Turn the Hands Up at 4 Oclok and wash Cloase. At 2 Bells after 4 Oclok Watch on Deck and Idlers Scrub and wash Uper and Main Decks. Up all Hammocks at 4 Bells. Pipe to Breakfast at 5 Bells. After Breakfast Watch Below Clean Lower Deck. At 8 Oclock send up tagalant yards By the Hands. At 2 Bells Clean Guns. In the fornon General Quarters a firing at targats with shot. The Poop Party a firing ball at targats with thair minney riffels. Send Down the tagalant yards at Sunset. This afternoon we on rigged Davids. Leef for the watch untill tomorrow Morning. On the 9th A fine Morning. Morning Duty as Befor. After Breakfast watch below up all Mess things from the Lower decks to the Main Deck and Holey stone the Lower Deck. Loos sails at 3 Bells and fural sails at 7 Bells and Squar yards and Pipe to Dinner at 8 Bells. After Diner Pipe Down all Mess things. Clean arms and guns and Watch Below Holey stone main Deck. Watch on Deck Clean thair Sellves to go On Shoar On Leef. At 4 Bells thear was a Signal Made for the Vengeance to Prepear for Sea and we Knockd Off Holey Stoning the Main Deck and the Watch Of going a shoar. We Hoisted the Blue Peter at the formast and fired a Bigg Gun. Rigg the Deavids got in and up all Boats and send up tagalant and royal yards and Unmored ship. We got up one anchor and shortend In the Cabell of the Other.

April the 10th A fine Morning. Morning Duty as Befor. Pipe to Breakfast at 5 Bells in the morning watch. Divishons at 4 Bells in the fornoon watch. No Divine Servis. Pipe to Dinner at 7 Bells. Thear was one more Royal Marine joind our Ship yerterday. Thear was two gentilmen Cum On Board this Ship from London to Acompany Us to Malta. They Cum On Board this morning and the Captain Cum On Board about 1 Oclok and we sent Out all the Visiters and Up All Boats and Shorten in Cabell.

To Sea Again
We got our anchor up and Made sail And the Harbour Master Had took us Out sid Of the Breake Water by 5 Bells il the Afternoon with A good Breeze and a fair wind. We had Onley Our topsails and jib set at the time we Cum Out from the Sound. After we got out side of the Breake Water the Harbour Master Left Us and we soon Made Sail. We set tagalant sails and Courses and we Had a Leading Wind. And in the Evning Secure anchors. Fine all Night and a Light Breeze. On the 11th A fine

Morning. Watch on Deck Scrub and Wash Uper and Main Decks and set topmasts and Tagalant Studding sails. Lash (April the 11 1853) up Hammocks at 5 Bells. Pipe to Breakfast at 6 Bells. Call the Watch at 7 Bells and fifteen minits. Watch On Deck Fall in to Muster and Watch Below clean Lower Deck. Clean arms at quarter past 1 Bell. Quarters afterwards and Divishuns to put Down for Slops. Sum Part of the watch at Drill in the fornoon. Now we am under royals tagalant sails topsails and Courses and tagalant and topmast Studding sails. In the afternoon set Lower Studding sails. At 4 Oclok we was running 5 knots and the wind More A Beam. Up Cloase lines and serve Out Washing water. Runing West Southwest three Quarters west with the wind on Our Beam. Wash and scrub Cloase. During the night we Caried the Stabour 12th A fine Morning.

A Littell More Wind And It Shifted On Our Port Quarter and we set Port Studding sails and took in Stabourd Studding sails. In the afternoon at Bigg Gun Excersise. In the Evning after Quarters In all Studding sails and Shorten sail and Shift topsails in 7 minits and then set tagalant and royalsails. A Light Breeze. The wind on our Port Quarter runing West by Southwest by west One Quarter West going about 5 knots per Hour the same All Night.April the 13th A fine Morning. Watch clean Uper and Main Decks. Watch set Studding sails. The Breese freshond in the fornoon . Excersise for the Uper Deck Quarters of the watch. In the Afternoon the Main Deck Quarters at Excersise. A Good Breeze this Afternoon going from 9 to 10 knots Per hour.Stearing the same Cours as yesterday the Wind On Our Beem. In the first Dog Watch going 10 Knots Per Hour. After Super took In all the Studding sails and all Plain Sail took In and 1 reef in the Topsails. Going About 10 knots All Night.

On the 14th A fine Morning. Clean Decks as yesterday. In the fornon we was under tagalant sails topsails and Courses and then going 12 knots Per Hour. At 7 Bells we took in the second reef In the topsails and took In the tagalant Sails and Bracd up the yards. We am Forst to keep the Main Deck Sashes Shipt. Make and Mend Cloase. Our Cours is South South West. In the Evning Not so Much Wind. Set the tagalant sails. A Fair wind for us. It is on our Port Quarter. In the first watch Brase Up about 1 Point. On the 15th A fine Morning. Clean Decks and Shake Out 1 reef in the for and Main topsails and two in the Mizen topsail. General Quarters at 3 Bells in the fornoon watch and Beate the Retreate at 6 Bells. Clean Decks Afterward. Pipe to Diner at 12 Oclok. Call watch at 3 Bells. Fine all day. In the Evning we Shook Out all reefs and mend them And we Sited Land on our wether Bow. We am Stearing South South East. On the 16th A fine Morning. Holey stone Uper and Main Decks. After Breakfast Holey stone Lower Deck. In the Afternoon Holey stone the Main Deck again. In the Evning A Light Breeze but a Hevey Swell going from 4 to 5 knots Per Hour Stearing South Hallf South West. After Quarters to Divishons to ricive our Clean Hammocks to Sling them. A Light Breeze All Night. On the 17th A fine Morning. Watch Holey stone Upper and Main Decks. Lash up Hammocks at 5 Bells and Pipe to Breakfast at 6 Bells. Clean guns at 2 Bells in the fornoon. Beate to Divishons at 4 Bells. Divine Servis for the watch below afterwards. A Light Breeze all day. In the last Dog watch we weard ship and then we was Stearing North North West and all Most In A Ded Calm. Lightning and thunder all Night and we was Chessing the wind all Night.

On the 18th after 4 Oclok AM it Did rain the second Part of the Watch. Holey stone the Main Deck. In the afternoon the Lower Deck Quarters of the watch at Drill on the Main Deck. Scrub Hammocks and wash Cloase. In the first and Middell watches all Most In A Ded Calmn. April 17thA verey fine Morning. Haing up Scrubd Hammocks and Wash Cloase. After Quarters All the Small arm Men to Muster with thair arms. In the afternoon Pipe down Hammocks and wash Clean. In the Evning go to Divishons with Our Hammocks to return them and then reef topsails. We are Lighing East North East in all most a Ded Calmn. A Greate Deal Warmer Now than it was a Week A go. The Band Plais on the Aft Deck at 6 Bells in the afternoon to the Ward room Officers and about 6 Oclok PM on the Quarter Deck while the Captain is Dining. For the Ships Company our amusement is Is a Bangee on the Main Deck and 1 or 2 sets of Boxing Gloves on the for Caastell and singell stick in the gaing ways[28]. In the first watch we put the Ship A Bout and then we was stearing North North West. A Light Breeze.

On the 20th A fine Morning . First Hallf of the watch Scrub Main Deck Hornings and second Part of the watch Holey stone Main Deck and then scrub Uper deck. Bigg Gun Excersise in the fornoon. In the Afternoon we Put the Ship A Bout In All Most A Ded Calm. In the Evning we had a Littell More Breeze Going A Bout 6 knots Per Hour Stearing South by South East 1 Quarter South. A Verey Light Wind All Night. We Put the Ship About twice During the Night. On the 21st A Verey fine Morning. Holey stone Decks as usaral. At 2 Bells in the fornoon Watch the Sailors Had to Muster with thair Clows and Lashons and the Marines with thair side arms and Musketts and afterwards the Watch to Drill. Watch Below Make and Mend Cloase. Just Befor Diner we Sited the African Land. Stearing East North East. In the afternoon Air Bedding Lash Up Hammocks at 7 Bells in the Afternoon. After Suyper in almost a Ded Calm A Shift Jib. We Hav A Shifted topsails and Courses in Less time than we was A Shifting the jib this Evning. A Light Breeze All Night. In the first watch we Took Off our royals and Courses. Wash Cloase in the first and Middell watches.

On the 22nd A fine Morning and A Strong Breeze And About 4 Bells in the Morning watch we Entered the Gut of Gibralter with a fair wind and we steared up Opasite the town and Hove Two and send Away A Boate with Our Letters. And the Captain went On Shoar And He Cum On Board About 4 Bells in the fornoon watch and then we Put Out to Sea stearing with our royals and tagalant sails Topsails and Courses and all Port Studdingsails set stearing East by South and Had got a Fair Wind for Malta going 12 Knots Per Hour. After Super we took in royals and all Studding sails A Good Breeze all Night. Scrub Canvass in the middell watch. On the 23rd A fine Morning. Holey stone Uper Deck. After Breakfast Up All Mess things on the Main Deck and Holey stone the Lower Deck. After Diner Pipe Down all Mess things. Set the Stabeurd Lower and Main Top Mast Studding sails. Watch Holey stone Main Deck. A Verey Light Breeze. After Super In all Studding sails and reef topsails. We hav now On Her All Plain sail. Stearing East by south East. A Verey Light Breeze all Night. On rhe 24th A Light Breeze in the fornoon. Divine Servis for the Watch Below. We Hav alterd Our Cours 3 Points Stearing Now South East by East Standing toward the African Shoar. In the afternoon We Put the Ship About and run from the Coast of Barbary. We was Verey Cloas to the Land Befor we went About. In the Evning Reef topsails and we had A Strong Breeze Stearing North Hallf North East.

On the 25th A fine Morning. Clear Decks After Breakfast. Watch Shift Jib . Ware Ship in the fornoon. In the for and afternoon watch at Bigg Gun Excersise. In the Evning Hand Shift topsails and Courses and take In One reef In the topsails and we Complated It In 8 Minits. In the Evning all Most A ded Calm. Stearing East By South East allmost Deu East. In the first watch we had A Good Breeze Sprung Up and A fair wind with the yard A Braced Up a Littell all Night Going 8 Knotts Per Hour. Scrub and wash Cloase in the first and Middell watches April the 26th A Verey fine Morning. Holey stone Decks. We Squard yards befor Breakfast and After Breakfast set Lower and topmast Studding Sails and got A fair wind for Malta Stearing East By South East. In the afternoon the Wind Shifted A Hed of Us and we took In all Studding Sails and Bracd Up the Yards. In the Evning A Light Breeze Reef topsails. We Put the Ship About in the Last Dog watch. In the first watch about 10 minits to 12 Oclok we Bate for General Quarters Cast Loos the guns and load them and afterwards Sarch the guns and secure them and Pipe Down Hammocks and call the watch.

On the 27th A Fine Morning. Clean All Decks. In the fornoon Shake Out all reefs. A Light Breeze all day and a fair wind such as It Is. In the Evning Shorten all Plain Sails and reef topsails and make sail In the first and Middell watches A Good Breeze going about 8 Knots pr Hour. On the 28th A fine Morning. Holey stone Decks. After Breakfast the Breeze freshond And we took In the 3rd reef In Our topsails. At 12 Oclok the wind Spleet the Main topsail and we Onbent Him and Bent another In

Its plase. A strong Breeze all day. Stearing East By North East About 2 Points of our Cours to Notherd. Scrub and wash Cloase in the first and Middell watches. Rain All Night. April the 29th A weet Morning. A light Breeze. Shake out 2 reefs set tagalant sails. Rain all the fornoon No General Quarters to day. We hav Bracd In 3 times and Hav a fair wind Now. Fine in the afternoon In the Evning A Strong Breeze And We took Off Her Main Sail and reeft topsails. Rain at times all Night. On the 30th A Littell Rain . Holey stone Decks. Under forsail and forstaisel and 2 reefs in our top-sails. At 3 Bells in the fornoon watch we was under the Island Gallata. Squar yards. A Good Breeze Stearing South by East. At Diner time we Had Lime Dues Servd Out to Us As we Hav Bean On Salt Pervishons for 18 or 20 Days. A Light Breeze. In the Evning at 6 PM we was Opasite Pantalina Island Stearing East by South East with our Yards Squar. Sling Clean Hammocks this Evning. A Light Breeze All Night.

On the first of May A fine Morning. Holey stone Decks. Divine Servis in the fornoon for the Watch Below. A Verey Light Breeze all day the wind shifted from Our Port Beam to Our Stabourd Beam the yards Bracd up sharp. We am going Our Course . A Littell More Breeze Sprung Up In the Evning.May the 2nd A fine Morning. Scrub and wash Decks. A Light Breeze. The wind Shifts Very often. After quarters Squar yards and then we Hav a Littell More Wind and we Set all sails and we was Stear-ing South by East. We Had Lime Duse Servd Out to us at 6 Bells in the fornoon at 12 Oclok in All Most A Ded Calm. After Super Hands Shorten and Furell Sails and After Loose and and reef topsails. In the Last Dog watch thear was A Littell More Breeze Sprung up and we servd Out Washing Water and Pipe Scrub and wash Cloase in the first and Middell watches. In all most a Ded Calm all Night. On the 3rdof May a fine Morning. Clean decks. A Light Breeze all day. In the afternoon set all Studding Sails. In the Evning we got Opasite Gaza. At 6 Oclok Squar yards and then we was Opasite Malta Harbour. A Light Breeze.

We had Lime Duse Servd Out To Us at 6 Bells.This Evning Shorten all Sail and we Layi two all Night. On the 4th A Verey fine Morning. Scrub and Wash Decks. At 3 Bells thear was a A Steamer Cumming Out of Harbour On the 4th at 4 Bells Short-en and Furell Sails and Squar yards. At 5 Bells *the Inflaxabell* took us in tow and we got to Harbour about 8 Bells and Mored Ship and we got out Som of the Boates. Serve out Lime Duse in the fornoon. In the afternoon On Bent all sails and Send Down galant and royal yards and Hands out Launch. We wear white trowsers to Day. In the Evning Clear Beef Boate (?)Watering Ship all day. Leff for the Petty Of-ficers to go A Shoar untill 9 Oclok this Evning. On the 5th A fine Morning. Turn the hands up at 4 Oclok AM. Holey stone Uper and Main Decks and Staiing the Mast and setting up the riggen and getting in and stowing away Pervishons. We Hav this Evning Complated 4 Months Pervishons. We Hav Had fresh Meate to day. We Hav

Bean On Salt Pervishons for the Last 21 Days. On the 6th A Weet Morning and It Did thunder and Lightning Verey Much. Scrub Hammocks and Haing them up and Scrub and wash Decks. In the fornoon the Purcer paid 2 Months Shoart Alowance Money to the Ships Company. The Poart watch got 44 Hours Leave to go On Shoar. Getting in Coals and ree stowing booms in the afternoon.

May the 7 A Verey fine Morning. At 4 Oclok Call the watch. Holey stone Decks. Painting the Inside of the Ship in the Afternoon. All the Ships In Harbour On Bent All Sails. Now In Harbout Is the *Brittania Trafalgar* 3 deckers, *rodney Belerophon Albion and Vengeance* 2 deckers, and *the Arethusa* friget and 2 or 3 more steam frigets, and 3 or 4 more Paddell Wheel Steamers. On the 8th A fine Morning. Call the watch at 4 Oclok. Scrub and wash Decks .Divine Servis in the fornoon. After Dinner Leef for the Starbourd Watch to go On Shoar untill the 10th Morning 8 Oclok. I went A Shoar then and Cum Off on the 10th. But on the 9 Morning, A fine Morning and thear was One Of Our Marines Found Dround Ashoar. He Had A Hallf a Sovering and sum Silver In His Pocket. When He was found He was Quit Ded[29]. On the 10th A fine Morning. Verey Hot All Day.

On the 11th A fine Morning. At 8 Oclok sent up tagalant yards. At 9 Oclok Bent for and Mizen topsails and afterwards Excersise new raise Men and Boys and all the fleet Dun the same as Us. May the 12thA Verey fine Morning. Holey stone Uper and Main Decks General Quarters in the fornoon Air Bedding In th afternoon. On the 13th A fine Morning and All Day. Marines at Drill In the fornoon On Board and Make and Mend Cloase in the afternoon. In the Evning after Supper Shift tagallant mast, All of Us. The flag Ship Complated in 5 Minits and 30 seconds, and *the Arethusa* in 5 Mins 40 seconds, Us in 5 Minits and 50 sds . And all the reast was longer than that, And afterwards bent topsails And We Was First By Far at that. On the 14th A Littell rain in the Morning, Holey stone the Uper Deck. In the Morning watch after Breakfast Pipe up all Mess thingsfrom the Lower Deck to the Main Deck, and Holey stone the Lower Deck. We hav Dinner on the Main Deck to Day. After Dinner pipe Down all Mess things again. Holey stone the Main Deck.In the Evning to Divishons for our Clean Hammocks. On the Morning of the 15 We Slung Clean Hammocks. Holey stone the Uper and Scrub the Main Deck. Send up the tagallant yards at 8AM, Divishions at 4 Bells and Divine Servis afterwards. Very Hot All Day. Fural Horning after Supper. Down tagallant yards at Sunset.

On the 16th A Verey fine Morning. Wash Decks as youseral. Send up tagallant yards at 8 AM. Spread All Uper Decks Horning. After Quarters, Stations for to Man and Arm Boats. Fine all day. After Quarters in the Evning Pipe fural Horning and Away All Boats for a pulling Match, *the Britanias* and Ours. On the 17th A Verey fine Morning. Turn the Hands up at AM and Scrub Hammocks, fine to dry them. Excersise with Sails to day all the Ships In Harbour. Thear was a Meraican steam frigit Cum In to Harbour Last Night and She Saluted the English Flag and then Saluted the Admirals flag and the Admiral returnd Hur A Salute. On the 18th fine all day. Exersise spars and sails all day. On the 19th A fine Morning. The Admiral Cum On Board at 5 Bells in the fornoon. He Musterd the Ships Company and we Beat to Geanerrel Quarters and when He Left the Ship He went On Board His Own Ship *the Britania*. In the afternoon all the Marines Had Orders to Land to Morrow morning to Drill. May the 20th A fine Morning and all the Ships Marines in Harbour Landed About 7 Bells in the Morning Watch. We was Drilled on Felorean Drill ground and we returnd to Our Ships About 4 Bells in the fornoon Watch. Thear was about 12 or 13 hundred went On Shoar. At 7 Oclok the Admril and all the post Captains Dined On Board Our Ship, and thear was a play On Board the admrials ship this Evning[30].

On the 21st A fine Morning. Clean Decks. In the Evning thear was 4 or 5 post Captains Dined On Board This Ship. On the 22nd A weet Morning, after 8 fine. Divitions and Divine Servis In the fornoon. Leff in the afternoon. On the 23rd A fine Morning. Send up tagallant yards at 8 AM and afterwards we got Our Best Bower Anchor and Cabell Up all Boats and all the reast of the Ships the same. At Sunset send Down tagallant yards. On the 24th A fine Morning. Call the watch at 1 Bell after 4 Oclok AM. At 8 Oclok send up tagallant yards and Dress Ship. At 6 Bells in the fornoon watch all the Marines Belonging to the fleet Landed on Valetta side and just Befor 12 Oclok All the Ships Mand yards. At 12 Oclok they all fired A (May the 24, 1853) Royal Salute and gave 3 Cheers. All we Marines and 3 Regmints was formed in line. After the Shipping had Dun Saluting we Fired A futersjoy (feu de joie) 3 rounds Each Man and then we Marched round the Parade Ground in reevew Orders and then formd in line and Marchd to the frunt and Halted and gave A genaral Salute. It was A Verey Grand Sit. Thear was a greate Maney People to see it 3 or 4 thousand. We got On Board about 4 Bells in the afternoon watch. At Sunset On Dress Ship and send down tagallant yards. On the 25th A Verey fine Morning. Excersuse with Spars and Sails all day. On the 26th A fine Morning. Man and Arm Boats and Fired 3 rounds. In Launch and the Marines that was In Her fired 3 rounds with thear Muskets and then return On Board. Send Down tagalant yards at Sunset.

On the 27th A Verey fine Morning. Turn the Hands up at 4 AM .Clean Decks And we got in 1 Hundred tuns of Water. We Hav Complated 4 Months Pervishons To Day. In the Evning fural Horning.(awning) After Quarters He made a signal for us all to Bend and fural topsails and Courses and Hed sails and Spainkers. We Compleated All of Ours in 6 Minits and 30 seconds. Sum of them was 14 Minits At It. On the 28th A fine Morning. Holey stone the Uper Deck and wash the Main Deck and Holey stone the Lower Deck. To Day we Hav Bean getting In Sheep and fowells for the Officers sea stock and Sum More Water To Day. On the 29thA fine Morning. Call the watch at 4 Oclok AM. Watch Holey stone Uper Deck. At 8 Oclok up tagalant and royal yards Divine Servis in the morning. The 30th A fine Morning and after Breakfast we was Hozen Ship and all the fleet the same. At Sunset send down royal yards. On the 31 Call all Hands at 4 Oclok AM. Scrub and wash Cloase. Exersise with sails to day.

On the Gloreyest 1st of June 1853 A Verey fine Morning and all Day. On the 2nd of June A Verey ..... Morning. Clean Decks in the morning watch. In the fornoon genearal Quarters. After Dinner Aire Bedding and In the Evning Pay Shoart Alowance Money the Ships Company. On the 3rd A fine Morning. Scrub and wash Cloase, fine all Day. Seirve Out tobaco and Soape to the Ships Company this afternoon. On the 4th Holey stone All Decks. At 8 AM Loose sails, fine all day. Sling Clean Hammocks .In the Evning Leff for the Watch to go On Shoar untill to Morrow Morning. On the 5th A fine Morning. *The Vulcher* Steamer left this Harbour with Invalides to take to England about 1 Bell In the morning watch. And there was a steamer Brought Out admril Stward to relave admril Harvey admril of the Dock yard and He was Salutid By the foarts and By the Shipping. Divine Servis in the fornoon. In the Evning Not Send Down the galant yards Non of the fleet. On the 6th A Verey fine Morning send up royal yards and (June the 6th 1853) Loos Sails at 8 Oclok AM. Exersise with sails all day. Pipe Hands to Bathe in the Evning.

On the 7th A fine Morning. Turn the Hands Up at 4 Oclok AM and Scrub Hammocks and wash Cloase fine to dry them. And after we had returnd our Hammocks we went to Divishons with them and returnd them and just then thear was A Steamer Cum In Hear from Constantinople And She Had Sum News For Our Admril[31]. That was in the Evning and Befor 8 PM he fired a Bigg gun and we got In Our Boom Boats. On the 8th turn the Hands Up at 4 Oclok Am and got things redey for towing. Pipe to Breakfast at 3 Bells and at 5 Bells We Slipt Our Morings and a Steamer took us in tow and towed us out side of the Harbour and all of us Made sail. We am Stearing East by South East from Malta with a Good Breeze and a Fair Wind. Now together thear is 2 ,3 Deckers 4 ,2 Deckers 1 friget and 5 Steamers. On the 9th A Verey fine Morning But a Verey Light Breeze. Out all reefs in our topsails. Stearing East 1 point South East. Geareal Quarters in the fornoon . A good Breeze all the afternoon. In the Evning after Super Shift Mizen topsails and Courses. We Dunit in 4 Minuts and we was the first Ship In the fleet and the Admril made a Signall to Us Very well Executed Vengeance. On the 9th a fair wind In the first watch

But in the middell watch rain.

On the 10th morning at Oclok fine. At 5 bells in the Middel watch the admril Made A Signall for Us to make all possabill sail and so We Did and soon past By all the reast of them but twas not Long Befor we Lost all the wind we Had. At 8 Oclok in all most A Ded Calm at 12 Oclok a Littell More Breeze and thear was steamers took all the reast in tow, But we keept ahed of them. Then at 5 Oclok the Admril Made a signal for Us to Shorten sail and at 6 Oclok *the Sampson* steamer Cum and took us in tow. At 3 Bells in the Middell watch the admril Made a signall to furall saills. On the 11th A fine Morning. Holey stone Decks. In the fornoon *the Niger* Steamer Broke Down thear was sum thing the Mater with Her Engines. Thear Hav Bean 2 more steamers join us sines we Left Malta. Thear is 7 steamers with Us Now. In the fornoon A Light Breeze But Very Hot. We am now Between the Greekish lands at 12 Oclok stearing North East by North. In the Evning after Super reef topsails. Stearing North East by East. At 12 Oclok we Entred the Durow Passidge at 5 Bells in the Middell watch. On the 12th A fine Morning . Make sail in the Morning watch Divishons at 3 Bells and Divine Servis afterwards. In the Evning make sail and set all studding sails and then reef topsails and Shorton sail and Now we am stearing North East by East under topsails and Sum times under tagalant sails and royals. Hoter to day than we Hav found it this Sumer. We past By Vola Bay this Evning. We am to the North East of Vola Bay and am Stearing North East.

On the 13th A fine Mornong and at 6 Bells in the fornoon we past by Tridados and at 8 Bells the steamers Let go of us and we Dropt anchor In Becika Bay and then the Consul went On Board the flag Ship and Ours and then Changed Saluts. On the 14th A fine Morning. And then the Consul Left Hear for Constantinople. Scrub and wash Cloase and Decks. Hot all day. This Evning the french fleet Cum In to this Bay and Dropt Anchor and Fired a Salute to Us and then we returnd the Compliament. The french hav got in this Bay Now 3 three deckers and 5 two deckers and 4 Steamers. This Evning *the Carrodock* Cum In Hear from Constantinople. On the 15th A fine Morning and we sent away the Launch and 2 pennaces A shoar for Fresh water. We left Malta on the Wednesday and got Hear on the following Monday And it is about 1 Hundred Miles . We Hav got 15 Ships and Steamers and the french Hav 12. 27 all to gether . We Hav Fild Up with water to day. This Evning all of our Captains Had A Invatation to go On Board the french Shipping to Dine and so they Did . June the 16thA fine Morning. To day On the 17th A fine Morning the french Officers Cum On Board of our Shipping and Dined in the Evning. Thear Have Bean A Merican Friget Cum Down from the Dardinells to day. Bathing in the Evning. On the 18th A fine Morning the furies Steamer In Hear from Gibralter and she Cald at Malta and Brought Our Mail to Day. Thear Hav Bean another French admrial joind thair Fleet to Day. Thay Hav 3 Admrials In thair Fleet Now. On the 19 A fine Morning. Our Captain so Sick Now. The french Had A Nother Steamer joind them to day. In the Evning It Did thunder and Lightning Verey Much . On the 20th A fine Morning. At 8 Oclok AM Dress all our Shipping And all the french at 12 Oclok fire a royal Salute and all of the Shipping .On Dress Shipping at Sunset. Sines we Hav Been Here the turks Hav Landed at Constantinople 12 hundred troops from Alexandria. In the Evning All the Captains and Officers Dined On Board of the French Admirals ships. On the 21st A fine Morning Watering Ship to day. 2 Steamers past By Us to day with the Egyptian Troops. Bathing In the Evning.

On the 22 A fine Day. Excersise with spars and sails to day. We Hav fresh Meate the first time sines we left Malta. On the 23rd A fine Morning to day. There Hav Bean 2 More Steamers Cum In to this Bay. They Had One Admril In One of them and a Comodore in the Other. Thay was turks. June the 24th A fine Morning. Scrub and wash Decks Make and Mend Cloase. To Day the English and french Admirels Dined On Board the turkish Admrials Ship and this Evning the turkish admrial Left Hear for to Join thair fleet at Alexander. Thay Do Belong to the Grand Turks. On the 25th A Verey fine Day and Verey Hot Winds When thear is any. We am filling up with Coals to day. Bathing in the Evning. On the 26th at 4 AM rain Verey Hevey. Today thear Hav Bean 1 french and 1 turkish steamers Cum in Hear with troops from Alexander to go Up the Black Sea. No Divine Servis to day for the Chaplin is Still Sick. On the 27th A fine Morning and we Hav Got In 40 tons of water to day. On the 28th A verey fine Morning. Excersise with sails. And the 29th A fine Morning and the 30th A Verey fine Morning. In the afternoon air Bedding.

On the 1st of July A fine Morning. Bathing in the Evning. On the 2nd of July A Verey fine Morning and All Day. Bathing in the Evning. On the 3rd A Verey Fine morning and on the 4th A Verey fine Morning. And on the 5th A Verey fine Morning. Hands Scrub and wash Cloase. On the 6th A fine Morning. A Watering Ship and A Painting the Main Deck to day. On the 7th A fine Morning. At 8 AM thear was A Boy floged for theft. Excersise with sails. Fine all Day. July the 8thA Verey fine Morning, Excersise with Sails and Make and mend Cloase to day and Thear is Many A Thousand of Locusts Cum from the Shoar. They Cums in Clouds. We foarcd to keep sum Hands on the Uper Deck all the time A sweeping them Up and Fling them Over Board. On the 9th A fine Morning. Excersise with Spars and Sails by Day and Bathing in the Evning. On the 10th Call the watch at 4 Oclok AM. Scrub and wash Decks and thear Have Been Another Steamer pass By Us to go up in the Black Sea. She is A Loaded with Egyptian troops. Today we Hav sent off 1 steamer to Marsells and 1 to Malta with Despatches for England to go By the Over Land Mail. On the 11th Waterig Ship. On the 12th A fine Morning. Hands Scrub and wash Cloase. At 4 Oclok AM

Bigg Gun Exersise to day. Serve out Slops to the Ships Company. On the 13th A fine Morning to Day. Thear Hav Been Another Egyptian Steamer go up In to the Black Sea with Troops. In the Evning our admrial and the french admrial and all of the Post Captains Dined on Board the rodney. On the 14th In the fornoon our Admrial and Sum of our post Captains went on Board *the Caradock* Steamer and she took them up the dardanells and they Returned in the Evning.

On the 15th A fine Morning. One of the french admrials Hav Been retiared to day But For What We Canot Say. Watering ship today and Saluting with Bigg Guns and french hav a nother 3 Decker join thair fleet to day. July the 16th 1853. A fine Morning, and all Day. Holey stone all decks to day. On the 17th A fine Morning. Divishons in the fornoon and in the Evning Load Boats with Emty Casks to go On Shoar tomorrow for fresh water. On the 18th A fine Morning. Call away the watering Party at 4 Oclok AM to go a Shoar for fresh water and they did not Cum Of untill the first watch and we unloaded them . And in the first watch thear was A Steamer Cum from Malta and She Brought Out Our Mail and Sum Pervishons for Our Ships from Malta and We got It On Board the Same Night or the next Morning. On the 19th A fine Morning. Scrub Hammocks and wash Cloase. A Strong Breeze All Day. On the 20th Away all Boats for fresh water at 3 Oclok AM and call the watch at 4 Oclok AM. And at 4 Bells in the morning watch the admrial Made a signall to Bent all small sails. And at 8 Oclok AM He made a signal to send up tagalant and royal yards and Loos and Make All Sail. And we all set Studding Sails Lower and A Loft and we was the First Ship by 3 minits and 20 secunds and the friget was the Next to us. In the Evning we got out our 2 Pinnaces.

On the 21st A fine Morning. In the morning watch *the Montublar* 3 Decker french Ship Waid anchor and Made Sail and Left the Fleet and Stood Out to Sea. On the 22nd A fine Morning. Watering Ship to day. Bathing in the Evning. On the 23rd A fine Morning Scrub and Holey stone all Decks and Exersise All Sails. July the 25th 1853 At 8 Oclok AM Spred Uper Deck Horning and at 4 Bells the Captain reid Prairs. At sunset send down the galant yards. On the 25th A fine Morning. Call away the Boats to go On Shoar for fresh Water. Watch pick Oakum. Clearing Boats with fresh Water. On the 26th A fine Morning. Picking Oakum. Send down tagalant yards at sunset.

On the 27th A fine Morning. Excersise with Sails. One of the french 3 Deckers Got Up Her Anchors and Made Sail and stood towards the dardanells and about 6 Oclok PM She got Ashoar about 1 ot 12 Miles from Us. In the First Watch All of the French Steamers got Up thair Steam and went out to thair Ship that was A ground But they Could Not get her off. On the 28th A fine Morning. General Quarters. In the fornoon Air Bedding. In the afternoon Our Captain Is Verey Ill In His Cabin. Thear Hav Bean 5 or 6 steamers of the French Out A Long Side of that ship that is Ashoare triing to Get Hur Off But She is Hard and fast Now Ashoar at Sunset. July the 29th 1853. A fine Morning. Call all Hands at 4 Oclok AM. Scrub and wash decks. Getting in fresh water to day. The french ship is Ashoar still. In the Evning we bend Sheet Cabel. Our Captain is worse to day. On the 30th A verey fine Morning. We hav got in sum Bred &Salt Pervishons. Our Captain is Very Bad Now. The french Ship is Hard and fast still. She was Making 30 Inches of water Per Hour This Morning . They Hav Bean A Clearing Evry thing Out of Her to day. On the 31st A finr Morning. Our Captain is Verey Bad Now. Thear is 2 Dockters with him Most of the time. In the Evning He Is Rather Better So thay Say. The french Ship is on the rocks Still But thay Swang her to day but She got in the sam Posation A Gain. Her name is *the Fresiland*. On the 1st of August ....

For whatever reason, and tantalising as it may be for us, from this point on no personal record of Willcox Webb's experiences exist. Nevertheless it is possible to reconstruct from other sources the circumstances in which he would have found himself over the next few years.

Experience of War

In November 1853 Russian warships destroyed the Turkish squadron in their own base at Sinope on the Black Sea. The British and French fleets entered the Black Sea in January 1854 and the Crimean War was declared at the end of March. In the beginning it was a popular war at home. The declared object was to defend Turkey against imperialist Russia (i.e. to prevent her gaining direct entry into the Mediterranean!) The fleet under Admiral Dundas on *Brittania*, with Admiral Lyons on *the Agamemnon* as his second in command, sailed through the Bosphorus into the Black Sea. Incidentally Lyons' flag captain was the John Mends who was made Post Captain on leaving the *Vengeance* at Plymouth in 1853. The allied armies were assembled at Varna on the coast of Bulgaria where they stayed until late in the summer. Ominously there was already a heavy incidence of cholera among the French troops. Admiral Lyons cruised with a squadron that did not include *Vengeance* along the Circassian coast. The British and French fleets (nine English and seven French ships of the line, plus frigates) blockaded Sebastopol. In early September -- too late in the year -- the troops were embarked for the Crimean peninsula, landing at the Old Port just south of Alma town. There was no opposition from the Russians to the landing which took several days and involved the naval brigade in unremitting toil. Their cheerfulness and strength impressed everyone. The Alma was hardly an ideal site for a landing, being described as "a muddy little creek only some thirty yards across".

Fortunately the weather was very calm, at least in the early stages, and this meant that the *Vengeance* had to be towed by a steamer (a procedure that I feel Webb always regarded as an indignity). There were signs already of the lack of forethought and organisation that was to bedevil the campaign but by the 18th September the army had established a foothold and were ready to attack the Russian positions. The Royal Marines took no part in the fighting at this stage but Webb, like everyone else, was soon to discover what war really meant.

The battle of the Alma was hailed as a glorious victory. Morale was high and certainly the French and British fought bravely as did theTurks although it was noted that they showed no mercy on the enemy wounded. By some accounts the Russian troops behaved badly by turning on their captors after surrender. Russian wounded were even known to attack medical orderlies or British soldiers offering them water. This was in part because they had been led to believe that they could expect no mercy and that they would inevitably be ill treated.

There were very heavy casualties and for two or three days after the engagement the field was still strewn with dreadfully wounded men. Their removal to a place of safety and what medical care could be provided was largely the task of those who had come through the battle unscathed and of sailors and marines from the fleet. The dead were to be buried and the wounded carried down to the beach where they were embarked on warships and transports and conveyed to the hospital at Scutari, itself to become notorious for its inadequacy. The horrific sight of the massive injuries and cruel disfigurements of the wounded, their desperate need for water and the agonies that they suffered while being moved, with the sheer physical effort of carrying them (for no stretchers were provided except those that the sailors improvised themselves) shocked and dismayed everyone concerned. J.W.W. would have been no exception. Army doctors did their best but were totally overwhelmed. Their field stations had much in common with abattoirs. On board of the ships that were used for evacuation every space was taken up by five hundred or more wounded. The stench was appalling, there were maggots and gangrene, and some of the men were also suffering from cholera. There was virtually no medical care available. Only those who had witnessed such a scene could fully comprehend the horror. It was inevitable that the experience had some effect on our farmer's son. It may well have altered him forever.

The next development in the course of the war was that, rightly or wrongly, instead of pressing home their advantage and attacking Sebastopol from their present position the army were ordered to march around the flanks of the city through a countryside ravaged by the Russian army to Balaclava. The fleet sailed parallel to them down the coast. The little port of Balaclava was south of the town itself. It was quite landlocked, three quarters of a mile long and three or four hundred yards wide, deep enough to provide shelter for even large ships. There was very little resistance to its occupation. On arrival they were presented with a very pleasant prospect. As Christopher Hibbert puts it in his excellent and superbly researched book *The Destruction of Lord Raglan* ....

"Everywhere there was fruit for the picking. Poultry could readily be bought by the officers and stolen by the men. Water was plentiful and so was hay and firewood. Midshipmen roamed happily about the harbour shooting geese and ducks." [32]

The ships were well supplied, fresh vegetables were available. Conditions were quite pleasant at this point.The health of the allied forces improved and with it their morale. Unfortunately this war was not to "be over by Christmas" and the army was not prepared for the Crimean winter. Not only were the senior officers and Commanders lacking in field experience (it had been a long time since Waterloo) but the Commiseriat and the whole supply system was hidebound. The army could not long be supplied by local resources and already the position had begun to deteriorate. Cooperation between the allies and indeed between the individuals commanding different branches of the British forces was sometimes sadly lacking (a case in point being the personal antipathy that existed between Lord Lucan and Lord Cardigan).

Meanwhile the Russians were busily reinforcing the defences of Sebastopol which they believed to be unassailable. Willcox Webb would have been with the fleet, steaming South with the intention of bombarding the town from the sea. The Russians had sunk two large ships across the entrance to the harbour and this made it impossible to approach as closely as they would have liked. *Vengeance* was towed in by the *S.S.High Flyer*. To have much effect against the stone walls of Sebastopol naval guns would have needed a range of no more than 500 yds. In fact they were placed almost a mile away so were of no great use except to intimidate the population.

On Sept 29th a Naval Brigade was assembled under the command of Lt. Col. Thomas Hurdle for service ashore. Webb, being attached, according to his record, to the steamer *Rodney*, was among them. There were 1,000 sailors and 1,500 marines deployed and as usual they were given the task of hauling guns and ammunition to where they were required –on this occasion up a narrow valley to the Eastern Heights where they constructed redoubts for their batteries. They were sent to relieve and partly replace troops of the 1st Division commanded by Sir Colin Campbell. At the ensuing Battle of Balaclava three Turkish redoubts in the valley below were over run. The Russian heavy cavalry descended on the 93rd Highlanders who showed great courage and strength in holding them off. The marines opened fire with their heavy guns and were also able to hold their position. It is not a possibility from his position that JWW would have been in sight of the famous charge of the Light Brigade although no doubt he heard some lively discussion of it during the weeks that followed. Incidentally the casualty list for the battle of Balaclava includes ten men from *HMS Vengeance*, one of whom was another John Webb (which may account for our hero being known as John Willcox Webb in the service).

By this time Winter was approaching and conditions for the army were deteriorating fast. Contemporary descriptions and quotations taken from Christopher Hibbert's book *The Destruction of Lord Raglan* give a vivid picture of how the situation was to develop. As early as October ....

"The army returned to its unrelieved diet of salt meat and biscuits the very thought of which was enough to make a man with diarrhoea or dysentery feel sick. Balaclava itself had already become a stinking, congested shambles with ships packed tightly in the harbour like leaves in a blocked drain. Piles of stores, boxes, sacks, bundles of hay, lay in muddled heaps on the quayside and rubbish and refuse floated and stagnated in the water." [33]

It was absolutely tragic that the supplies of food, clothing, and other necessities were not forwarded to the units for which they were intended and where the need was so desperate.

"Bleached by the sun, shrunk by the rain, rubbed by equipment, used as bedclothes, torn by brambles, the clothes of many of them, worn continuously, were certainly not likely to last much longer."[34]

The army lay entrenched before Sebastopol, which they had hoped in vain to take before the long winter arrived. When it did it brought nothing but suffering to the wretched besiegers. As Sergeant Timothy Gowing of the Royal Fusiliers recalled....

"Every night covering parties crawled forward into pits beyond the batteries. It was killing work lying down for hours in the cold mud, returning to camp at daylight, wearing out with cold, sleepy and hungry – many a poor fellow suffering with ague and fever, to find nothing but a cold, bleak, muddy tent without fire to rest their weary bones in – and often not even a piece of mouldy biscuit to eat." [35]

When the Crimean campaign medal was awarded at a later date Webb was given clasps for Balaclava, Inkermann and Sebastopol. The Inkermann clasp was returned as "not entitled". We know from this that he must have missed this fierce and bloody battle but we can only guess at the reason for it. It is more than likely that he was incapacitated at the time. Cholera was rampant and conditions were to become so bad that it was a lucky man who survived without falling prey to that or some other infection adding to the misery that they were all forced to endure.

On November 14th, just after the battle of Inkerman, came the "Great Hurricane." The Marines were camped on the Heights above the harbour. As Hibbert tells us, quoting Paymaster Dixon among others....

"Everything went Whizz Bang in less time than I have taken to tell you. Tents leaped into the air and went flying over the plateau looking like bits of paper, stones were lifted from the ground and crashed into any obstacles that lay in their path, cutting men's faces, tearing into the sailing canvas, smashing bottles, ringing against cans. Great barrels could be seen bounding along like cricket balls. Heavy wagons were thrown headlong through the camps dragging bullocks after them as if they were mere kittens" Hospital marquees collapsed, their poles torn out of the ground and the sick were tossed in their muddy blankets helplessly across the ground".

"Midshipman Wood of the Naval Brigade, weak from diarrhoea, tried to crawl on his hands and knees toward the protection of a low wall surrounding some powder boxes ,but he was blown well past it and had to be dragged back by a Lieutenant and two sailors who scrambled toward him holding hands. When all four of them had got back to the wall they lay down beneath it." [36]

In the harbour conditions were as bad or worse and it may be that if Webb had been serving on a ship at that time he would have been in even greater danger. Fanny Duberly [37], on board *the Star of the South* watched while....

" the little clipper 'Wild Wave' rolling helplessly in the roaring breakers and three cabin boys left on its lurching decks trying to clutch at a rope which some other members of the crew on the rocks above threw down to them. Two of the boys were washed overboard and the third caught a rope and leapt ashore just as the ship fell down on a tumbling wave and disappeared in a scattered mass of splinters, broken masts, bales of cargo, hay and boxes".

At least eight transports were wrecked with all the desperately needed supplies that they carried (including forty thousand greatcoats and boots for nearly the whole army) and with great loss of life. This was a tragedy for men already near to starvation and having no decent clothing or shelter. Even worse was the condition of the cavalry mounts and draught animals. By November General Buller's A.D.C.was writing in a letter home....

"The horses and oxen for transport are either dead or too weak to work. In every direction they are to be seen dead or dying in the mud and our men, working more like beasts of burden than Christians, are floundering about up to their knees in mud. Three horses in each Cavalry regiment die on an average every night of cold and hunger. They have eaten each other's tails off. I saw a horse today eating a piece of canvas covered in mud." [38]

"Thousands of tons of supplies rotted in the stores and in the holds of ships while men struggled up through the mud past the rotting corpses of animals the broken carts, the dead and dying Turks, carrying on their backs the bare means of keeping alive." [39]

It was chaos. Raglan was driven to despair by the incompetence of Admiral Boxer, in charge of transport from Constantinople who kept no books or records. For weeks on end....

"ships lay outside Balaclava waiting to come in and unload and when they did so their crews, although well used to Eastern harbours were appalled. Since the storm the ghastly pale-green waters were like a stagnant cesspool into which all imaginable refuse had been thrown. Dead men with white and swollen heads, dead camels, dead horses, dead mules, dead oxen, dead cats, dead dogs, the filth of an army with its hospitals, floated amidst the wreckage of spars, boxes, bales of hay, biscuits, smashed cases of medicines, and surgical instruments, the decomposed offal and butchered carcases of sheep thrown overboard by ships cooks." [40]

"By the beginning of the second week in February scurvy was more or less prevalent in all regiments, and the men's teeth, loosened in their soft and spongy gums could not eat their biscuit until it had been soaked in water. Ten weeks before three steamers had come into the harbour loaded with vegetables but much of the cargo was already rotten on arrival and there was no means of getting the remainder up to the camps. Three thousand pounds worth of vegetables were thrown overboard. On 19th of December 20,000lb of lime juice arrived at the harbour but it was not until Lord Raglan called for a return of goods in store that anyone in authority seemed aware of its arrival. On 20th of January he ordered that lime juice should form part of the soldiers' rations." [41]

I cannot resist one more quotation from Hibbert's account of conditions during that dreadful winter. It adds to the realization of just how extreme the privations must have been even for officers. When Midshipman Evelyn Wood's boots gave out he gave a sailor ten shillings to find another pair in the Russian graves on Inkerman

Ridge. Many other officers and men followed his example and held on to them even after new ones arrived from England; for the new boots were not only of such shamefully bad quality *"the soles dropped off after a week's wear"* but many of them were far too small.[42]

The French forces were far better organised. The British army deserved better. I wish I knew what our Mendip farmer's son had to say about it all. If he wrote letters home they have not survived and he would hardly have had the means or the heart to keep a journal at this point. All that I know for certain is that he was there and suffered with the rest.

However, Spring did eventually come and with it fresh supplies of all kinds. The morale of the army improved with the season. The allies were still camped before Sebastopol and the taking of this strongly fortified town remained their principal objective. Its defences were under the direction of Todleben, a very talented Engineer Officer in the Czar's army. Of the 16,000 men who formed the garrison 12,000 were sailors as the Russian fleet (to the fury I might say of its officers) were penned in the harbour by those same sunken ships that were used to prevent the allies from gaining access. During the summer they were reinforced by 28,000 fresh (though inexperienced) troops. There was also the town's civilian population and refugees from the surrounding countryside. The strength of the walls and its advantageous position convinced the Russians that it could be held indefinitely and gave the allies some pause for thought. Todleben had constructed well placed redoubts for gun batteries and was well supplied with ammunition. The town was subjected to heavy bombardment on seven or eight occasions over the period between April and September of 1855 but no breaches were made that were not repaired overnight, and in response the Russian guns were equally busy. Apart from Inkermann, there were minor excursions and skirmishes but it was not until September 8th that the allies made a determined attack in which the French succeeded in taking the Malakoff tower. At the same time the British attacked the Redan, the other key strongpoint, under very heavy fire and across 200 yards of open ground. At great cost they succeeded in forcing an entry but had not sufficient men to hold it and were driven out. Nevertheless the French had penetrated the defences and the Redan had been compromised so the Russians very efficiently extricated themselves by evacuating their entire force during the night by way of a floating bridge across the river.

As Willcox Webb was granted the Sebastopol clasp for his Crimea campaign medal he was evidently actively engaged. Almost certainly he was serving the naval guns in the bombardment and probably helping to construct redoubts and trenches for shelter. Now however hostilities were drawing to a close and negotiations for an armistice beginning. On September 17th the Naval Brigade were ordered to rejoin the fleet. How very glad they must have been!

The Veteran

Webb was first sent on board the Royal Albert and then returned to England on the transport *Jura*. His final posting was to *the Royal Yacht Victoria and Albert II*. This may have been something of a reward for his years of hard and active service. The yacht was used by the Royal family to review the fleet at Spithead and also took a short cruise in the Mediterranean. *Victoria and Albert II* was a paddle steamer and was soon replaced by a screw ship, *Victoria and Albert III*. In the following year Webb received his discharge, having served for ten years. His conduct was marked down as "Good". I understand that this is not the highest praise possible and that he may have blotted his copy book somewhere along the line. I cannot think any less of him for that. He was a good man.

At the time of the 1861 census Webb is shown as living at Bennets Hill Farm again with his father Joseph, mother Mary, and sister Keturah. In 1881 his father has died though his 86 year old mother was still there. John was 57 and he had a wife now. Her name was Ann Elizabeth. Her age was given as fifty. They had been married for twelve years or more but there was no record of any children. There was also a neice, Julia Gunning, the daughter of his oldest sister Ann. Julia was recorded as a dairymaid. John was described as a farmer of 80 acres employing two men and a boy. Any man who survived the Crimean War and returned unscathed must be considered lucky. Now it was his turn to sit by the fireside on winter nights and talk of his adventures and memories – though there may have been some on which he did not care to dwell. John Willcox Webb's death was registered at Frome in the summer of 1882. I feel glad to have made his acquaintance, however indirectly.

Dinah Read

CONTEMPORARY ILLUSTRATIONS

The Royal Navy's blockade of Kronstadt was decisive in bringing the Crimean War to an end.

Saving the Guns

Commanders of the Allied Armies in the East

Camp of the English Light Division at Varna

'London Illustrated News' *artist on the Battlefield of Inkerman*

The Rifles and Royal Marines on the Heights at Balaclava

'Sane' & 'Sidon' *Allied Steamers on the Lookout Before Sebastopol*

The Naval Brigade dragging a heavy seige gun to the Green Hill Chapmans Battery.
Marine Webb would have been involved in such operations.

Sailors of Green Hill Battery Before Sebastopol.
Part of Marine Webb's duties would be defending the Battery from frequent Russian attacks from Sebastipol.

Florence Nightingale at the hospital at Scutari, a former barracks, unfortunately built over a sewer with disastrous consequences for the wounded.

Portion of the British Artillery Camp and seige train before Sebastopol

Shipment of wooden barracks aboard 'White Falcon' at Southampton for the French Army in the Crimea.
The improvement in the living quarters of the Allied army was as a result of public opinion and outrage.

Hospital in Sebastopol; Dr Durgan Tending the Wounded

The Baltic Fleet at anchor off Spithead. It was the Royal Navy campaign in the Baltic that eventually brought about the end of hostilities in the Crimea.

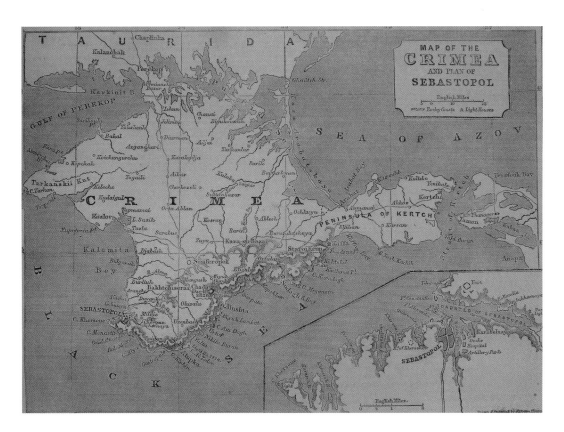

NOTES and SOURCES

1. The crucial importance of supplies of fresh food to the welfare of seamen cannot be over emphasised and was as much a factor at this time as at any other.

2. Top Gallant.

3. No doubt this was on account of what Webb calls "Brain Fever". It was vital to prevent the spread of fevers and infections in the fleet.

4. The number of instances in this narrative of falls from aloft, either overboard or onto the deck, may seem shocking but they were a principal cause of death on sailing ships and a constant danger.

5. Drills and training were undertaken whenever possible. The whole force needed to be in good fighting trim. It was noted that the Royal Marines and Naval Brigade subsequently did good service at Sebastopol and the Alma.

6. The tone of superiority and moral disapproval here is intriguing. J.W.W. never gave overt expression to emotion but it is plain that he regarded the Marines as an elite force from whom high standards are expected.

7. Competition, both on board and between ships, was important for the maintenance of efficiency and morale. J.W.W was evidently proud of his ship and her performance. The results of exercises and trials of sailing were always logged and may well have had a bearing on which ships were kept in Commission when cut backs were ordered.

8. This was the first real account in the journal of stormy weather. It indicates that the marines did play a role in the actual handling of the ship and were not merely seaborne soldiers.

9. Having run a ship aground was a nightmare for any captain and the efforts needed to get a ship off were desperate. Russell must have been very relieved to be able to reward his crew with an extra ration of rum in celebration of their success.

10. No doubt it is for this reason that the otherwise dutiful Webb lost his good conduct badge a week later. Overstaying leave was a constant disciplinary problem, as was desertion. They were often associated with drink. Sailors drew money from the purser to go ashore. It was quickly spent.

11. That is, about one bullock for about 450 men for one day.

12. This was the steam Frigate *Avenger*, wrecked on passage from Malta to Gibralter on Sorrelli Rocks off N. Africa. 245 out of her 250 men were lost.

13. Salt meat for thirty five successive days is an indication of just how monotonous the diet must have been. Lime juice had been served only toward the end of this period.

14. Friendly relations between the allied fleets were cultivated by social contacts and with due ceremony. One wonders what the crew made of it all.

15.Site of the last sea battle (1837) in which only sailing ships took part

16.*Vengeance* emerged from the Mediterranean into the wintery seas of the Atlantic. She had orders for home but was to call at Lisbon. Conditions were difficult and it was not easy to get into the Tagus.

17.*Vengeance* joined Admiral Curry's fleet. For some unknown reason Curry seemed set on making things difficult for Capt. Russell but the *Vengeance* gave a good account of herself – to Webb's satisfaction and no doubt to that of the whole Company.

18.*Phaeton* and *Vengeance* were Buddy Ships. They had respect for each other, even admiration.

19.In home waters for Christmas! The crew were allowed to celebrate in the traditional way although the death of a marine strikes a sad note. It often seemed to have happened that a sick man would struggle to survive and then depart peacefully once he knew he was back in home waters.

20.The ship was at home for an extensive refit of which Webb gave a full account. Officers and crew expected to get long leave in their turn but many of them were rebellious and impatient, as we shall see.

21.Mends was appointed to the *Agammemnon*, a steamship and served in her in the Crimea. He was a good officer and his successor found him a hard act to follow.

22.*Vengeance* was sent to Plymouth Dockyard to complete repairs and her refit. It was more comfortable than being anchored offshore in winter weather. The detailed account of this procedure is illuminating.

23.This near-mutiny was one of the few major incidents of resentment described by Webb. There might have been several reasons for the discontent. Many of the men may have had family in Hampshire and felt that though in England they were still separated. Others, Devon men, would have been equally impatient to get home leave. The new Commander was not much known to the men and seems to have imposed a very tight regime. Throughout the winter there were problems with absence, desertion, and discipline in general. The men were understandably restless and there was a lot of hard work required of them.

24.It is interesting to note that Webb's journey home was by rail but that it took some 48 hours with two or three changes and two overnight stops. At home he was glad to go to markets with his father and brother and enjoyed country sports etc. He makes no mention of his mother, which seems a little odd. His journey back to Plymouth was much swifter but he then spent some four days on shore. This meant that he overstayed his leave but he managed to avoid punishment by some kind of brinkmanship.

25.The struggle to maintain discipline and control would continue as long as the Captain was not on board. Not until *Vengeance* was ready for sea again did things settle down.

26.Another pointer to a certain laxity in the Captain's absence.

27.This curious procedure seems to have been a form of peaceful protest. It appears that a tough regime had been imposed which the crew regarded as unreasonable. It is to be noted that within a couple of days of this incident they were to revert to the old routine "As we Had Got when our Old Commander Had Got Comand Of Us".

28.*Vengeance* seems to have become a happy ship once again. Morale was much higher. It is also notable that Webb was much more seamanlike in his language than at the beginning of his service. He was now much more aware of the technicalities of sailing and even of navigation.

29.It was a common hazard for seamen to drown at the dockside while under the influence of drink, often being crushed between a moored ship and the dock wall.

30.Amateur dramatics were a popular distraction on warships, as were dancing and music making and competitions of all kinds. There was an air of excitement building up at this time and the whole fleet may have been in high spirits. There was a degree of pomp and circumstance with parades and friendly rivalry between ships.

31.This dispatch may have been for the Admiral's eyes only but it was often the case that the whole ship, even the whole fleet, had a fair idea of what was in the wind.

32.Hibbert *The Destruction of Lord Raglan* Longmans 1961.

33.Hibbert *The Destruction of Lord Raglan* P113.

34.Ditto.

35.Sergeant Timothy Gowing *Voice from the Rank*s ed Kenneth Fenwick 1954.

36.See Chapter13 Section 11 of *The Destruction of Lord Raglan* for a fuller account of the effects of the "Great Storm".

37.Mrs Duberly the wife of Captain Henry Duberley was a determined lady who resisted pressure from the authorities to stay at home. She was present throughout the campaign. She was known as the *Vulture* by the troops from the pleasure she seemed to take in riding over the field on the aftermath of a battle.

38.Quoted by Hibbert in Chapter14 P205 of *The Destruction of Lord Raglan.*

39.*The Destruction of Lord Raglan* P213.

40.Ditto P206.

41.Ditto P239.

42.*Destruction of Lord Raglan* P245.

Appendix 1

Ships mentioned in the journal:

Albion 2 Decker.
Arethusa 1850 Frigate.
Bellerophon 2 Decker.
Brittania 1820 Large 3 Decker, hulked in 1885.
Ganges 2 Decker.
Hercules ?
Indefatigable Frigate.
Phaeton 1850 Frigate. Later converted to steam screw.
Prince Regent 1812 Cut down to second rate and converted to steam screw.
Queen 1844 1st Rate.
Rodney 1836 90 guns 1st Rate. Capt. Graham
Sasparell ?
Superb 2 Decker.
Trafalgar 1st Rate.
Vengeance. First commissioned 1852. Pure sailing ship. 2 Decker. 85 guns.
        Fast and handy. Capt. Lord Edward Russell was at the bombardment
        of Sebastopol. *Vengeance* and *Rodney* were the last sailing ships home.
Victory 1st Rate. (Lord Nelson's of course) was used as a receiving and training
        establishment in Portsmouth at that time.

French Ships

Freiseland
Montublar ?

Steamers

Agamemmon 1853 Screw Steamer. Command of Capt. M R Mends (late of
     Vengeance) when made Post Captain.

Blazer

Encounter

Firebrand

Furey 1846 Bulldog Class.

Genius ?

High Flyer

Inflexible 1846 Bulldog Class.

Leopard 1859

Lynx Gun Vessel

Myrmydion 1844 was a flag ship in Cork, a steamer capable of 9-11 knots. Second
     class gun vessel. Iron built. Length 151 ft.

Niger 1846 Screw Ship.

Radamanthus was a hulk in Cork Harbour used as barracks. It was overcrowded
     and uncomfortable as quarters, complained of by officers and men.
     Transport 1841. Troopship1851. First R.N. steamship to cross the Atlantic.

Rattler Steam Screw.

Sampson 1844 Cyclops Class. Barque rigged with two funnels.

Sidon 1846 Refitted to carry troops.

Sphynx Paddle steamer.

Spiteful

Termagent 1854 Single Screw Steamer.

20 *Terrible* 1846 The largest paddle steamer built as a warship for the Royal Navy.
     Later served in the Far East.

21 *Tiger*

22 *Vigo* at Plymouth was a hulk moored alongside vessels undergoing refit.

Appendix 2

On Foreign Shore

Now he was free to go – at Liberty
With a high heart he stepped ashore and then
Stopped short and stared around him, eagerly
Taking it in – amazed by what he saw
Silvery twisted trees, and sun etched vines
Shading a lime washed couryard bright with flowers.
Brittle strands of sun parched grasses clung
To beaten hard baked earth and time smooth stone.
Tall leafless spires of chalk white stars arose
And golden whorls of spikes and prickly thorn
Straggled beside the road, new and unknown,
And from the hills drifted a hot dry wind
Blending the scents of thyme and spicy herbs,
And aromatic dark mysterious pines.
Strange, unfamiliar. He thought of home,
Saw in his mind a Mendip combe
Verdant and ferny, damp, the smell of earth,
Grey stones cushioned deep in creeping moss.
So Different. He shook his head. And then
Two golden girls came by with baskets on
Their hips, and slid a glance slyly toward
Our Volunteer. And joy washed over him.
"Our Dad," he thought, "Never saw ought like this!"

Dirty Weather

A nasty cross swell, and the brig
Groans as she plunges deep
From crest to trough, rolling most vilely.
The wind whines, drums and vibrates
Along her straining spars, shrieks
Through her taut black shrouds.
Her timbers work and grind.
She's making water sure.
Her sails storm jib and mizzen,
Certain they are to split
That or they drive her under!
Now her decks are swept
By massive weights
Of black and evil water.
God send she may not broach!
Rigid with terror our Marine,
Lips compressed and white with cold,
Clings to the ladder, drenched,
Fighting a panic that he dare not own.
Dawn light brings no relief.
A tearing sky, ugly and black,
The sea a maelstrom and the crew
As battered as the ship herself.
The weary helmsmen strive
To hold her on course,
Certain that one small error
Will betray them all.

Three days later,
Making good the damage,
Willcox Webb thinks he's
An old hand now,
Tested and tried, and true.
Their barkie, *Vengeance*,
Weathered the storm alright.
And so did he. Willcox Webb.

Bibliography

Author Uncredited: *The History of the Present War with Russia*. London Printing and Public Company, 1855.

Calthorpe, Somerset: *Cadogan's Crimea.* John Murray Ltd., 1856,1857,1858. 1979 Book Club Associates edition used. (Illustrated by Cadogan, George).

Gardiner, Juliet and Wenborn, Neil (Editors) : *The History Today Companion to British History*. Collins and Brown Ltd., London, 1995.

Hibbert, Christopher: *The Destruction of Lord Raglan (A Tragedy of The Crimean War 1854-1855).* Longmans, Green and Co. Ltd., London, 1961.

Godman, Temple: *The Fields of War*, edited by P. Warner, London, 1977.

Gowing, T: *A Soldier's Experience or a Voice from the Ranks.* Nottingham, 1895.

James, Lawrence: *Crimea 1854-1856.* Van Nostrand Reinhold Company, New York 1981.

Smith, Cecil Woodham: *The Reason Why*. Constable and Company Ltd., in association with The Book Society, 1953.

Picture credits

Page 2, National Maritime Museum; page 4, London Illustrated News; page 6, LIN ; page 8, LIN; page 10, Dinah Read; page 14, photographer unknown; page 15, Thomas Bewick; page 70 (bottom), W H Pyne; page 71, LIN; page 72, LIN; page 73, LIN; page 74, LIN; page 75, LIN; page 76, LIN; page 77 (top), LIN; page 77 (bottom) W H Pyne; page 81, Thomas Bewick; page 82, Thomas Bewick; page 85, W H Pyne; page 88, W H Pyne.

Dinah Read's Acknowledgements

First and foremost, I am deeply indebted to Douglas Watts for loaning me John Willcox Webb's journal which he had found amongst his family papers and allowing me to transcribe it. Ann Elizabeth Purnell whom Webb married after his return to Coleford was distantly related to him, both being descended from Fisher Purnell born in 1798. Douglas and his family have been generous and welcoming and have shown a continuing interest in the results of my investigations.

I would like to thank Len Barnett who carried out careful research for me at the National Maritime Museum in Greenwich and at the General Records Office in Kew regarding Marine Webb's service record and other matters relating to naval history in the 1840s and 50s and particularly in regard to H.M.S.Vengeance.

I also thank the volunteers at Radstock Museum for their help and interest, especially with the Webb family history and in locating their former homes and connections. I would particularly like to thank Julie Dexter for her cheerful encouragement and expert help.
My thanks also go to Danny Howell of the Warminster and Wylye Valley for Local Study, for information received from him.

Fiducia Press Acknowledgements

The staff of Bristol Central Reference Library.
Our thanks to Julie Cochrane of The National Maritime Museum, Greenwich.
Our thanks to Harrison Little of The Royal Marines Museum, Southsea.
Reproductions from *Thomas Bewick and his School*. (Dover Publications, New York, 1962).
Reproductions from *Rustic Vignettes for Artists and Craftsmen,* by W.H. Pyne. (Dover Publications Inc., New York, 1977.
Reproductions from *London Illustrated News* (Crimean War Period).

Fiducia Press is a non-profit making community publisher specialising in local and social history, transport and poetry. For a full booklist contact the address below or the Bristol Book Publishers website.

www.bristolbooksand publishers.co.uk